THE BEST OF
THE BEST OF
BROCHURE
Design

ROCKPORT

THE BEST OF THE BEST OF BROCHURE Design

BEVERLY MASSACHUSETTS

ROCKPORT PUBLISHERS

First published in the United States of America by
Rockport Publishers, a member of
Quayside Publishing Group
100 Cummings Center
Suite 406-L
Beverly, Massachusetts 01915-6101
Telephone: (978) 282-9590
Fax: (978) 283-2742
www.rockpub.com

ISBN-13: 978-1-59253-629-0
ISBN-10: 1-59253-629-8

10 9 8 7 6 5 4 3 2 1

Edited by: Rachel Hewes and Allison Hodges

Printed in China

contents

CORPORATE
AND ANNUAL
REPORTS

Spread (pages 2–3)

Simultaneously we sought to provide real alternative thinking and options, whether it was through covering holistic health, visionary human-potential-movement leaders, or solutions to social conditions proffered by local grassroots activists.

On the cultural front, first off we wanted to be a real writer's paper. Also, we had a vision of creating a home base for the unheard smart voices, the new visions, and the artistic creativity exploding in the community — for instance, we opened the pages to the power of the punk and new wave music movements and put together a remarkable team of movie reviewers.

A big part of the vision was to help forge a real citywide community out of what we found to be a collection of adjacent neighborhoods that scarcely knew about each other. We sought to show readers the richness of who they were, the wealth of remarkable places and people all around the L.A. basin, and the creative and intellectual juices actually surging here outside the entertainment industry. Our vision was extremely democratic — we wanted to be the people's hip paper that celebrated the rebel in everyone. We very much wanted to be a paper that people took personally because it had heart and soul as well as good information.
—Jay Levin, Founding Editor

2

20 YEARS OF *LA WEEKLY*

It's hard to imagine life in Los Angeles without the *LA Weekly*. Since the first edition appeared 20 years ago and over 1,000 issues ago, there have been millions of words, photos, ads, cartoons and illustrations; thousands of bands, movies, plays and books reviewed; popular and unpopular positions taken, readers moved and offended, lives and a city transformed. For a whole generation, it's always been there, letting people know what's happening, helping to define L.A., telling stories, offering opinions. And, like that first issue, it's still free.

3

Spread (pages 10–11)

LA Weekly's groundbreaking coverage of the conflicts in Central America, environmental issues and the local arts scene generated widespread publicity, won numerous awards and played a significant role in shaping the life of the city.

THE LIST OF L.A.'S FIVE MOST UNDERREPORTED STORIES OF '66 INCLUDED THE PERILS OF OVERDEVELOPMENT, THE AEROSPACE INDUSTRY'S WAR ON A PEACE ORGANIZATION, AND THE COUNTY'S AMBIVALENCE TOWARD THE NEEDY.

10

magazine called *L.A. Style*, edited by Joie Davidow. The magazine, the result of the fashion boom of the mid-'80s, catered to advertisers and readers who were already familiar with the *Weekly*'s format but wanted a glossy vehicle. During the mid-'80s, *L.A. Style* was one of the fastest-growing magazines in the country and winner of many design awards. In 1988, *L.A. Style* was sold to American Express Publishing.

Throughout the 1980s, *LA Weekly* continued to cover the city — and the nation and the world — from an alternative point of view. Its groundbreaking coverage of the conflicts in Central America, environmental issues and the local arts scene generated widespread publicity, won numerous awards and played a significant role in shaping the life of the city. In-depth articles on politics, on poverty and race, on culture, which could not be found in any other publication, caused elected officials to respond and citizens to become active.

In 1988, as Jay Levin became involved in other

11

Spread (pages 4–5)

The *Weekly* would cover the offbeat in L.A., not by those pointing a touristic finger and saying, "Oh, isn't this odd?" but by those who lived it.

ON THE EVE OF THE CALIFORNIA NUCLEAR FREEZE INITIATIVE CAMPAIGN, THE WEEKLY PROFILED A LEADER OF THE ANTI-NUCLEAR WAR MOVEMENT AND A SURVIVOR OF HIROSHIMA.

CONTINUING IN ITS COVERAGE OF THE BURGEONING HOLISTIC HEALTH MOVEMENT, THE WEEKLY PROFILED FOUR L.A. HEALERS WITH DISTINCTLY DIFFERENT METHODS.

4

Jay Levin, a journalist who was editor of Flynt Publications' *L.A. Free Press* when it folded in 1978, had a vision of Los Angeles as a disparate group of towns that could be linked together and galvanized by a newspaper like the *Weekly* — one that would inform readers all over the city about what was going on in the arts, politics, movies and music. The *Weekly* would cover the offbeat in L.A., not by those pointing a touristic finger and saying, "Oh, isn't this odd?" but by those who lived it. It would create a sense of community among the myriad local neighborhoods.

After the demise of the *Free Press*, Levin approached local businesses and entertainment figures for their support of a new weekly paper in L.A. Actor-producer Michael Douglas and entrepreneur Pete Kameron were among the original investors in the project and remained on its board of directors for many years.

In November of 1978, with Jay Levin as editor, Joie Davidow as Calendar editor

5

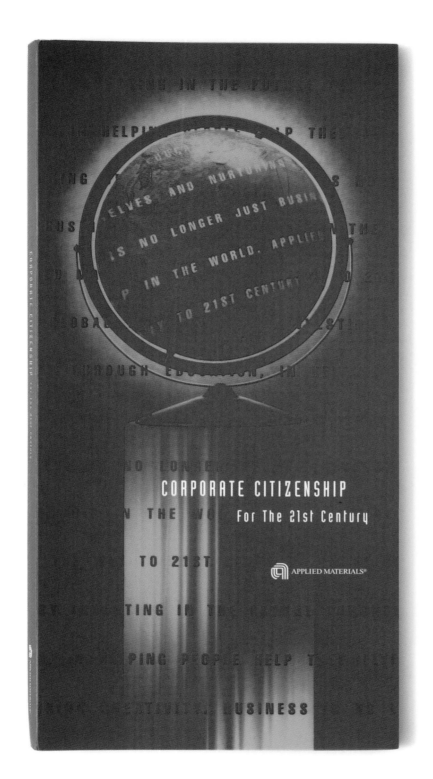

CORPORATE CITIZENSHIP
For The 21st Century

APPLIED MATERIALS®

DESIGN FIRM > Melissa Passehl Design
ART DIRECTOR > Melissa Passehl
DESIGNER > Melissa Passehl
PHOTOGRAPHER > Robert Cardin
COPYWRITER > Susan Sharpe
CLIENT > Applied Materials
TOOLS (SOFTWARE/PLATFORM) > Macintosh, QuarkXPress
PAPER STOCK > Starwhite Vicksburg
PRINTING PROCESS > Four-color PMS

DESIGN FIRM › Country Companies Design Services
ART DIRECTOR › Tracy Griffin Sleeter
DESIGNER › Tracy Griffin Sleeter
PHOTOGRAPHER › Stock Photography
COPYWRITER › Greg Martin
CLIENT › Agency
TOOLS (SOFTWARE/PLATFORM) › Macintosh
PAPER STOCK › Frasier
PRINTING PROCESS › Offset by original Smith printing

The Big Dance
Hyatt Regency San Diego
San Diego, California
June 30 – July 5, 2001

What better way to reward your efforts than a trip the entire family will enjoy - to beautiful San Diego, California? If you've never been there, or haven't been there for awhile, you'll be amazed how much there is to do and see.

San Diego is an excellent place the whole family can enjoy. If you're looking for a wild time, you'll find three of the wildest just minutes away – Sea World, Wild Animal Park and the world-famous San Diego Zoo. Looking to enjoy the weather? Rent some bikes, skates or kayaks and soak up the sunshine on Mission Bay or along any of the city's 70 miles of beach.

If golf is your game, you'll like what San Diego County has to offer - 50 public courses to challenge all levels of golfer. From desert landscapes to country hillsides to

views of the Pacific, San Diego has it all, including Torrey Pines Golf Course - home of the Buick Invitational.

Want something a little more relaxing? Enjoy lunch at one of San Diego's ocean-view restaurants. Go antique shopping, stroll the boutiques or take a quiet walk along the beach at sunset. Finish off the day in Gaslamp Quarter, where you'll find one of the city's liveliest nighttime street scenes.

Of course, what would July 4th be without a picnic and fireworks? Following a picnic with all our Big Dance qualifiers and their families, enjoy a front row seat to fireworks right from the grounds of your hotel - the Hyatt Regency San Diego, located on San Diego Bay.

Fun for everyone – that's what San Diego has to offer. And it's a fitting reward for making it to The Big Dance.

Here's how you do it:

Qualification Criteria

Contest Period:
December 1, 1999 -
November 30, 2000

Requirements
Agents: Must be ranked in Top 640, based on Contest Credits
Must have produced at least 48 Contest Units

Agencies: Must be ranked in Top 64, based on Contest Credits Earned
Must have met at least 90 percent of Contest Unit Base

Experience Factors
Contest Credits vary, based on the length of time a person has served as a Country Companies agent, as shown below. These factors will also impact the agency's Contest Credit totals.

Agent Experience (As of 12-1-1999)
Contest Credits Received
Basic Needs Agents
125% of Contest Credits Earned
8-12 months
120% of Contest Credits Earned
13-24 months
115% of Contest Credits Earned
25-36 months
110% of Contest Credits Earned
37-48 months
105% of Contest Credits Earned
More than 48 months
100% of Contest Credits Earned

The Big Dance.

That's what fans call the NCAA Division I tournament. And whether they say so or not, everyone who loves college basketball wants to make it there. Little else matters. Because regardless of the success a player, coach or team enjoys, they all dream of making it to *the dance.*

It's a reward for a year's worth of focus and effort. It's about talent and heart and making sacrifices others did not. It's about doing what it takes to rise above the rest. It's about fulfilling a dream and earning the *National Champion's ring.*

This year, we're introducing our own version of **The Big Dance.** It, too, will reward focus, heart and sacrifice. It, too, will be about fulfilling dreams.

Are You Ready to Play?

At the end of each NCAA season, 64 teams are invited to 'the dance.' Once the tourney begins, the field quickly narrows. *From 64 to 32, from 32 to the "Sweet Sixteen," "Elite Eight" and "Final Four."* The battles end only after the *National Champion* has been crowned.

In our dance, agents and agencies will compete during a yearlong contest. At the conclusion, we will rank all agents and agencies based on their performance. The **top 640 agents and 64 agencies** meeting our contest requirements will earn their invitation to **The Big Dance** and participate in our **National Tournament.** We'll host two very special **All Star trips** for all agents and managers meeting our midyear qualification requirements, too.

Here's Your Letter

We've attached your letter to this book, to help serve as a reminder of your goals during this contest. Each step of the way, from **All Star** to **The Big Dance** and beyond, we'll award a special pin to all that qualify. It's a mark of distinction shared by a select few...those who pay the price to be among the best.

Here's Your Playbook

This book contains everything you need to know about **The Big Dance.** How the contest works. How to earn your invitation. And most importantly, all the great prizes you can win along the way if you've got what it takes to make it to the dance. *Interested?* Take a look inside to learn more.

a conscium business

DESIGN FIRM > Michael Courtney Design
ART DIRECTORS > Mike Courtney, Scott Souchok
DESIGNERS > Mike Courtney, Scott Souchok
PHOTOGRAPHER > Stock, Kevin Latona
COPYWRITER > The Frause Group
CLIENT > Vulcan Northwest
TOOLS (SOFTWARE/PLATFORM) > Freehand, Photoshop
PAPER STOCK > Potlatch McCoy
PRINTING PROCESS > Four-color offset

THE COTTON CENTER IS 280 ACRES OF EXTRAORDINARY BUSINESS OPPORTUNITY.

STRATEGICALLY LOCATED LESS THAN FIVE MINUTES FROM PHOENIX SKY HARBOR INTERNATIONAL AIRPORT, THE COTTON CENTER PROVIDES INCOMPARABLE ACCESS TO THE ENTIRE PHOENIX METROPOLITAN AREA.

BECAUSE THE COTTON CENTER IS IN THE CENTER OF THE REGION'S FREEWAY SYSTEM, MORE THAN 95% OF THE POPULATION OF AMERICA'S SIXTH LARGEST CITY LIVES WITHIN 40 MINUTES OF THE HEART OF THE COTTON CENTER.

THE AFFLUENT AND FAST-GROWING COMMUNITIES OF SCOTTSDALE, TEMPE, AHWATUKEE, CHANDLER, GILBERT AND MESA ARE WITHIN 20 MINUTES OF THE COTTON CENTER.

ARIZONA STATE UNIVERSITY, WITH ITS RENOWNED UNDERGRADUATE AND GRADUATE SCHOOLS, RESEARCH FACILITIES, BUSINESS INCUBATOR PROGRAMS AND THINK-TANKS IS ONLY 25 BLOCKS AWAY. 19 ADDITIONAL INSTITUTIONS OF HIGHER LEARNING ARE WITHIN 20 MINUTES.

THIS IS NOT YOUR TYPICAL COMMERCIAL REAL ESTATE. THIS IS THE VERY DEFINITION OF A PREMIER BUSINESS COMMUNITY.

DESIGN FIRM > After Hours Creative
ART DIRECTOR > After Hours Creative
DESIGNER > After Hours Creative
ILLUSTRATOR > Rick Allen
COPYWRITER > After Hours Creative
CLIENT > Cotton Center
TOOLS (SOFTWARE/PLATFORM) > Macintosh G4, Adobe Illustrator

:Boeing
737 — 800

BASIC AIRCRAFT SPECIFICATION

Maximum Take-Off Weight	174,200 lbs. (79,010 kg.)
Seating Capacity	12 First Class / 150 Tourist Class or
	186 Tourist Class
Galleys	G1, G2, G48
Engines	CFM56-7B27
Thrust	27,300 lbs.

P O W E R

A I R C R A F T

~italized and well-respected, we are
~eliver on our commitments.

DESIGN FIRM > Hornall Anderson Design Works, Inc.
ART DIRECTORS > Jack Anderson, Katha Dalton
DESIGNERS > Katha Dalton, Ryan Wilderson, Belinda Bowling
PHOTOGRAPHERS > Boeing, West Stock, Tony Stone, Alan Abramowitz
COPYWRITER > John Koval
CLIENT > Boullioun Aviation Services
TOOLS (SOFTWARE/PLATFORM) > QuarkXPress
PAPER STOCK > McCoy, Strathmore

Every year over a million Silicon Valley residents turn off their computers and go in search of adventure and romance.

They go on vacation. To Europe. Mexico. Hawaii. The Caribbean. And every other corner of the globe.

This large number of travelers, and their passion for the road, makes Santa Clara County the most lucrative travel market in Northern California.

DESIGN FIRM › Cox Design
ART DIRECTOR › Randy Cox
DESIGNER › Randy Cox
COPYWRITER › Mike Furnary
CLIENT › San Jose Mercury News
TOOLS (SOFTWARE/PLATFORM) › Photoshop, QuarkXPress, Macintosh
PAPER STOCK › French
PRINTING PROCESS › Offset

1999 Special Advertising Features of the San Jose Mercury News Sunday Travel Section

DESIGN FIRM > Hand Made Group
ART DIRECTORS > Alessandro Esteri, Giona Maisrelli
DESIGNERS > Alessandro Esteri, Giona Maisrelli
ILLUSTRATOR/PHOTOGRAPHER > Alessandro Esteri
COPYWRITER > Verdiana Maggiorelli
CLIENT > Tessile Fiorentina
TOOLS (SOFTWARE/PLATFORM) > QuarkXpress, Photoshop
PAPER STOCK > Zanders
PRINTING PROCESS > Printed in Pantone

DESIGN FIRM > Gee + Chung Design
ART DIRECTOR > Earl Gee
DESIGNERS > Earl Gee, Qui Tong
PHOTOGRAPHER > Stock
COPYWRITERS > Tracy Harvey, Susan Berman
CLIENT > Netigy Corporation
TOOLS (SOFTWARE/PLATFORM) > QuarkXPress, Adobe Illustrator, Photoshop
PAPER STOCK > Springhill SBS C25 24 pt., Appleton Utopia, 65 lb. cover
PRINTING PROCESS > Offset lithography, die-cut cover

DESIGN FIRM > The Bonsey Design Partnership
ART DIRECTOR > Chris Lee
DESIGNER > Damien Thomasz
PHOTOGRAPHERS > Andrew Hun, Alex Ow
COPYWRITER > Jane Cotter
CLIENT > Transtel Engineering
TOOLS (SOFTWARE/PLATFORM) > Macintosh, Freehand, Photoshop
PAPER STOCK > Matt art card
PRINTING PROCESS > Five-color plus one special

DESIGN FIRM > Fossil
ART DIRECTORS > Tim Hale, Stephen Zhang
DESIGNER > Stephen Zhang
ILLUSTRATORS > Ellen Tanner, Paula Wallace, John Vineyard, Jennifer Burk, Andrea Haynes
PHOTOGRAPHER > Dave McCormack
CLIENT > Fossil
TOOLS (SOFTWARE/PLATFORM) > QuarkXPress, Photoshop, Illustrator, Macintosh G3, Power PC
PAPER STOCK > Fox River Protera
PRINTING PROCESS > Four-color offset

DESIGN FIRM > SamataMason, Inc.
ART DIRECTOR > Greg Samata
DESIGNER > Steve Kull
PHOTOGRAPHERS > Sandro, Marc Norberg, Mark Craig
COPYWRITER > Laurence Pearson
CLIENT > Tupperware Corporation
TOOLS (SSOFTWARE/PLATFORM) > QuarkXPress, Macintosh
PAPER STOCK > Fox River, Coronado Vellum, Fox River Sundance, Canson satin
PRINTING PROCESS > Offset, sheet fed

DESIGN FIRM > Bloch + Coulter Design Group
ART DIRECTORS > Hollie Hory, Thomas Bloch, Ellie Young Sutt
DESIGNERS > Hollie Hory, Thomas Bloch, Ellie Young Sutt
PHOTOGRAPHER > Jerry Garns
COPYWRITER > Paul Losie
CLIENT > Amwest Insurance Group, Inc.
TOOLS (SOFTWARE/PLATFORM) > Macintosh, QuarkXPress, Photoshop, Illustrator
PAPER STOCK > Editorial: Potlatch Karma 100 lb. text; Flysheet: French Parchtone cream 60 lb. text,
Financial: Beckett embossed enhanced silk 80 lb., text
PRINTING PROCESS > All but cover sheet fed, hand bound with Acco fastener

DESIGN FIRM > Cross Colours Ink
ART DIRECTOR > Janice Beddington
DESIGNER > Janice Beddington
ILLUSTRATOR/PHOTOGRAPHER > David Pastoll
CLIENT > Nando's Chickenland
TOOLS (SOFTWARE/PLATFORM) > Macintosh, Freehand, Photoshop
PRINTING PROCESS > Lithography

to our shareholders:

At AptarGroup, we are committed to fulfilling the wants of consumers by making life simpler, more convenient and more efficient through better designed packaging solutions. For consumers, our dispensing systems make medicine easy to administer, fragrance bottles attractive and ketchup containers trouble free. Our innovation, diversified product line and continued geographic expansion have allowed us to meet changing consumer needs and have made us the preferred supplier of many of the world's best known companies. We are committed to what our shareholders want as well – excellence, long term profitability and growth.

In our seven years of existence as a free-standing public company, our sales have grown from $412 million to $834 million, a compounded growth rate of 12 percent. Our diluted earnings per share have more than kept pace with this growth, increasing at a compounded rate of 17 percent* over the same period.

Having successfully completed several strategic acquisitions in 1999, and having achieved record financial results in spite of challenging market and economic conditions, we are confident that AptarGroup is positioned better than ever to continue this tradition of growth as we enter the new century.

* Excluded from this figure are the effects of a change in accounting for income taxes in 1993, favorable lawsuit settlements in 1998, and a write-off of in-process R&D in 1999.

DESIGN FIRM › SamataMason, Inc.
ART DIRECTORS › Pat & Greg Samata
DESIGNER › Kevin Krueger
PHOTOGRAPHER › Sandro
CLIENT › Aptar Group
TOOLS (SOFTWARE/PLATFORM) › QuarkXPress, Macintosh
PAPER STOCK › Appleton–coated Utopia one, dull; Monadnock Aastrolite vellum
PRINTING PROCESS › Offset, sheet fed

DESIGN FIRM > Edelman Public Relations Worldwide

ART DIRECTOR > Mary Ackerly

DESIGNERS > Rosanne Kang, Lana Le

PHOTOGRAPHERS > Josef Astor, Whitney Cox, Doug Levere, Peter Loppacher, William Vasquez

COPYWRITER > Various

CLIENT > Barnes and Noble

TOOLS (SOFTWARE/PLATFORM) > QuarkXpress, Adobe Illustrator, Macintosh

PAPER STOCK > Mohawk 50/10

PRINTING PROCESS > Offset lithography

swift response

Quick and Nimble.
Meeting the Needs of the Network
Equipment Industry.

InNet Technologies was formed in 1995, at a pivotal time in the networking and telecommunications industries when new products were moving quickly to market, and contract manufacturers were expected to react instantly to ever-changing requirements. At the same time, product costs had to be constantly reduced.

The company's founders, who cumulatively share nine decades of experience in the design and manufacture of interface products incorporating magnetic components, created a plan to excel at meeting those needs. That plan has succeeded admirably and has propelled InNet to its present position as the most responsive and innovative producer of superior quality network interface components at the lowest costs.

Today, InNet's planning, product design, prototyping and sales and marketing activities are centered in its San Diego headquarters. Its Far East logistical center is located in the New Territories of Hong Kong; four manufacturing plants comprising more than 140,000 square feet, are located in Dong Guan, PRC, China.

InNet's rapid growth and financial stability is enhanced by its alliance with Stewart Connector Systems to develop a broad line of interface modules integrated within quality RJ-style connectors. Stewart's parent, Insilco Technologies, acquired a minority position in InNet several years ago. Together, the companies are rapidly making these "products of the future" the design choices of today.

DESIGN FIRM > Lorenz Advertising
ART DIRECTOR > Arne Ratermanis
DESIGNER > Arne Ratermanis
ILLUSTRATORS/PHOTOGRAPHERS > Arne Ratermanis, Michael Balderas
COPYWRITER > Carm Greco
CLIENT > InNet Technologies
TOOLS (SOFTWARE/PLATFORM) > QuarkXPress, Illustrator, Macintosh
PAPER STOCK > Potlatch McCoy Gloss
PRINTING PROCESS > Four-color litho with dull and gloss varnish; embossed cover

ART DIRECTOR:
ALESSANDRO
ESTERI

DESIGNER:
GIONA MAIARELLI

PHOTOGRAPHER:
ALESSANDRO
ESTERI

CLIENT:
LANIFICIO DEL
CASENTINO

SOFTWARE AND
HARDWARE:
QUARK
MAC

MATERIALS:
FEDRIGONI

PRINTING:
OFFSET

HAND MADE GROUP
LANIFICIO DEL CASENTINO
CORPORATE PROFILE

ITALY

LAVA GRAPHIC DESIGNERS
WERKELIJKHEID (REALITY)

ART DIRECTOR:
YKE BARTELS

DESIGNERS:
YKE BARTELS
DAAN JANSSENS

PHOTOGRAPHER:
ROYALTY-FREE
STOCK PHOTOS

CLIENT:
SIGNUM

SOFTWARE AND
HARDWARE:
ILLUSTRATOR
QUARKXPRESS
MAC G4

MATERIALS:
CHRONOLUX

PRINTING:
RIJSER

Una stagione dedicata alle seduzioni tattili
A season dedicated to tactil seductions

BY ANGELO USLENGHI

filtrate **PREZIOSITA'**

perfette **LEVIGATURE**

Visione attraverso una grata di un interno esotico-coloniale. Penombre e sfumature, luci soffuse, luminosità discreta, riflessi dorati. Aspetti setosi, mescolanze di lucido e opaco, fluidità e leggerezza. Minuscoli armaturati ed intrecci a canestro.

FILTERED PRECIOUSNESS.
View of an exotic-colonial interior through a grid. Semi-darkness and shades, soft lights, discrete brightness, golden hues. Silky appearance, mixture of bright and mat, fluidity and lightness. Tiny weaves and basket weaves.

colori **MATERICI**

CLASS

Le gamme colore si rifanno ai cromatismi presi da sostanze e materie alquanto inedite.
Gessosi. Colori impuri che richiamano i colori della calce, gesso, stucco, sabbie, pietre.
Cosmetici. Colori delle polveri e creme da make-up Tonalità epidermiche e tocco metallico polverizzato.
Preziosi. Colori scuri, filtrati,

ombreggiati. L'oriente nei toni delle penombre: i violacei, i blu, i beige dorati.
Bucolici. Colori olfattivi. Un bouquet di fiori, erbe, piante presi da orti e giardini.
Energetici. Colori forti ispirati dal mondo pubblicitario, dal dinamismo moderno e da folklori latini.

MATERIAL COLOURS.
Colour shades with chromatisms of substances and materials that border on the unusual.
Chalky. *The impure colours of lime, chalk, putty, sand, stone.*
Cosmetics. *Powder and make-up colours. Skin-deep hues and a powder metal touch.*
Precious. *Dark, filtered,*

shadowy colours. Oriental semi-dark hues: purples, blues, golden beiges.
Bucolic. *Olfactory colours. A bouquet of flowers, herbs, vegetable and flower gardens.*
Energetic. *Bright colours inspired by the world of advertising, modern verve and Latin folklore.*

armonie **BOTANICHE**

seduzione **TATTILE**

aspetti **ARTIGIANALI**

E' sicuramente una stagione all'insegna dei piaceri sensoriali dove il tatto acquista sempre più importanza. Le sensazioni più innovative provengono da mischie plurime di fibre: lana/seta/mohair, cotone/lino/lana e dall'uso di prodotti ausiliari inediti come il lattice, il silicone, il Teflon. Inoltre i finissaggi completano il risultato tattile con l'utilizzo di enzimi, sabbiature, lavaggi 'stone'.

SEDUCTIVE TOUCH.
This is certainly a season under the banner of sensory pleasures where touch becomes increasingly important. The most innovative sensations come from multi-fibre blends such as wool/silk/mohair, cotton/linen/wool and from unexpected auxiliary products such as latex, silicon, Teflon. Enzyme and sandblast finishes, "stone" washing give the final touch.

Natura vegetale in mostra. Aspetto delavato, tinture organiche. Raffinata semplicità. Freschezza e cromatismi presi da giardini in fiore. Armature semplici come tela, canvas e panama. Disegnature con leggeri riquadri da fazzoletti d'epoca.

BOTANIC HARMONIES.
Natural plant life on display. Washed-out appearance, organic dyes. Refined simplicity. Freshness and shades from blossomed gardens. Simple weaves such as in cloth, canvas and panama. Old-handkerchief patterns with light window panes.

Imperfezioni volute, superfici irregolari, aspetti granulosi. Rilievi e rugosità con uso di filati grossi alternati a filati sottili. Una nuova rusticità contenuta e raffinata con fondi leggermente crépe.

HANDICRAFT APPEARANCE.
Hand-made imperfections, uneven surfaces, grainy effect. Reliefs or roughness obtained with alternating coarse and fine yarns. A new restrained and refined rustic look with slightly crepe backgrounds.

ITALY

ART DIRECTOR:	DESIGNER:	CLIENT:	SOFTWARE AND	MATERIALS:	PRINTING:
ALESSANDRO ESTERI	GIONA MAIARELLI	LANIFICIO DEL CASENTINO	HARDWARE: QUARKXPRESS MAC	FEDRIGONI	OFFSET

INTERVISTA/INTERVIEW
Alfio Aldrovandi
DIRETTORE GENERALE DEL LANIFICIO DEL CASENTINO
GENERAL MANAGER OF LANIFICIO DEL CASENTINO

ORE **8** DEL **MATTINO:**

PRONTO SIGNORA WILSON, MI SENTE SIGNORA WILSON?

rivisitati

Basic modernizzato.
Ritorno a tipologie tradizionali
re-interpretate. Disegnature
spesso in bianco e nero ma
con interventi tecnologici.

CLASSICS REVISITED.
Modern basics. Traditional
reinterpretations return. Frequent
black and white motifs with
technological additions.

News

Our second issue One hundred and fifty
years Anniversary The market at the
millenium's end Trends for Spring Summer
'99 The new collection at Prato Expo
Vogue Tessuti on Lanificio del Casentino
Oliviero Toscani on Utopia and other
projects Interviews. And more…

ROSE DESIGN ASSOCIATES
TELEVISION CORPORATION
CORPORATE BROCHURE

The Television Corporation is the UK's leading independent supplier of programmes to broadcasters worldwide. Combining two of Britain's largest production companies, Mentorn and Sunset+Vine, with one of the UK's most respected production facilities operations, The Television Corporation is a fast-growing media business. The Group produces over 3000 hours of television each year for all the UK's major television channels, distributing them to around 200 countries . . . . . .

ART DIRECTOR:	DESIGNER:	PHOTOGRAPHERS:	CLIENT:	SOFTWARE:	MATERIALS:	PRINTING:
SIMON ELLIOTT	SIMON ELLIOTT	PAUL ZAK	TELEVISION	ILLUSTRATOR	VALLIANT GLOSS	OFFSET LITHO
		LOL KEEGAN	CORPORATION PLC	PHOTOSHOP	ART	
				QUARKXPRESS		

UK

ART DIRECTOR:
CHERYL WATSON

DESIGNERS:
CHERYL WATSON
SHARON McKENDRY

CLIENT:
TARGET

GRAPHICULTURE
TARGET BRAND BOOK & DVD

ART DIRECTOR:
CHRISTOPHER LEE

DESIGNER:
KAI

CLIENT:
UTS FAMILY MOVERS

SOFTWARE:
FREEHAND
PHOTOSHOP

MATERIALS:
MATT ARTPAPER

PRINTING:
4C X 4C

SINGAPORE

FABIO ONGARATO DESIGN
ARNOLD BLOCK LEIBLER
2002 YEAR IN REVIEW

WHAT REALLY
MATTERS IN
A LAW FIRM?

WHERE
THE RICH
TOO COME
FOR ADVICE

OUR RESULTS
SPEAK FOR
THEMSELVES

HELPING CLIENTS
THROUGH TAXING
TIMES

RECONSTRUCTING
AUSTRALIA'S
LARGEST
CORPORATE
COLLAPSES

CLIENTS'
RIGHTS:
MAINTAINED,
DEFENDED &
ENFORCED

INAUGURAL
AUSTRALIAN
LAW
AWARDS
WINNER

AUSTRALIA

DESIGNER:
RYAN GUPPY

CLIENT:
ARNOLD BLOCK
LEIBLER

ART DIRECTOR:
ANDREW GORMAN

DESIGNER:
ROB RICHE

PHOTOGRAPHERS:
PAUL DIXON
ROB RICHE
JOHN EDWARDS

CLIENT:
GALLAHER GROUP
PLC

SOFTWARE AND
HARDWARE:
PHOTOSHOP
QUARKXPRESS
MAC

MATERIALS:
MANNO ART MATT

PRINTING:
6-COLOR LITHO
CTD CAPITA

RADLEY YELDAR
GALLAHER ANNUAL
REPORT 2000

Gallaher Group Plc
Annual Review and Summary
Financial Statement 2000

USA

DESIGNER:
BRANDON MURPHY

PHOTOGRAPHER:
VARIOUS

CLIENT:
BELLWETHER
EXPLORATION

SOFTWARE AND
HARDWARE:
QUARKXPRESS
MAC G4

MATERIALS:
DULCET/FRENCH

PRINTING:
WILLIAMSON
PRINTING

SALTERBAXTER
SOUND PRACTICE

UK

Eco-efficiency
Using fewer resources, and wasting less of those we do use, makes economic as well as environmental sense.

COMPARED TO 1995, WE NOW USE 33 PERCENT FEWER SOLVENTS AND GENERATE 45 PERCENT LESS HAZARDOUS WASTE AND 32 PERCENT LESS POLYCARBONATE SCRAP FOR EVERY UNIT OF PRODUCT THAT WE MANUFACTURE.

SOUND PRACTICE

The Christian Music Group (CMG) in the US has reduced by two-thirds the standard number of samples it orders for every new release. It has also changed its procedures to ensure that any samples that still remain surplus to requirements can be booked back into stock. This will significantly reduce product waste in the CMG offices.

4

Our impact
All aspects of our business use resources and create waste. Manufacturing is an area where we have undertaken formal reviews of the impacts resulting from this, and closely monitored our performance against some key indicators.

Our manufacturing sites use raw materials including polycarbonate, aluminium, solvents and inks. We continually strive to improve the efficiency of the process and minimise the quantity of material which is wasted, at the same time reducing the environmental impact caused by the wastes.

Some waste is inevitable. A proportion of the solvents used are emitted as vapours; these can present a health hazard in the working environment and contribute to smog formation when released to the atmosphere. Water-based effluents are treated on site and then discharged to sewer for further treatment. Any waste that can't be recycled, including hazardous waste, is sent for external disposal at landfill sites or incinerators.

We also use ozone depleting substances across our businesses, in air-conditioning and some fire protection systems. If released, these substances will damage the ozone layer.

Our performance
Solvents
We made good progress in solvent reduction, achieving a 31% drop in the quantity used and a 24% reduction per million units output (pmuo). This was significantly better than our target reduction of 5% pmuo.

The improvements were mainly due to a change of solvent specification at Uden (Netherlands) and improved controls at Jacksonville (US).

Hazardous waste
We reduced hazardous waste by 7%. This was equivalent to a 3% increase pmuo and fell short of our target 10% reduction pmuo. The main reason for this was the deferral of a new waste water treatment plant at Uden (now installed).

Polycarbonate efficiency
Procedural improvements at Toshiba-EMI (Japan) and Jacksonville contributed to a 16% reduction in polycarbonate scrap, equivalent to 10% pmuo. This was better than our 5% reduction target.

Ozone depleters
We record purchases of ozone depleting substances. No CFCs or halons were purchased. Purchases of HCFCs, used to maintain existing units or install new ones, increased by 5%. We also purchased 170kgs of HFCs as replacements for HCFCs. These gases are ozone friendly but have a high global warming potential.

5

ART DIRECTOR:
PENNY BAXTER

DESIGNER:
IVAN ANGELL

ILLUSTRATOR:
IVAN ANGELL

CLIENT:
THE EMI GROUP

SOFTWARE AND
HARDWARE:
QUARKXPRESS
MAC

MATERIALS:
CYCLUS OFFSET

PRINTING:
LITHO +
LETTERPRESS

From 1993 to 2001:
In the charts and behind the scenes

93 94 95 96 97 98 99 00 01

02 03 04 05 0

SOUND PRACTICE

1

'Altijd groeien'

> REPLY ON Date: maandag, 25 februari 2002 11:09

SVB
Persoonlijke
ontwikkeling
Plezier
Samenwerken

THE NETHERLANDS

ART DIRECTORS:	DESIGNERS:	PHOTOGRAPHER:	CLIENT:	SOFTWARE AND HARDWARE:	MATERIALS:	PRINTING:
TIEMEN HARDER YEW-KEE CHUNG	TIEMEN HARDER YEW-KEE CHUNG	STAFF OF SOCIALE VERZEKERINGSBANK	SOCIALE VERZEKERINGSBANK	PHOTOSHOP QUARKXPRESS MAC	INVERCOTE ALBATO 250GSM + OXFORD 120GSM	OFFSET, 4-PROCESS COLORS

Sociaal Jaarverslag 2001 > Sociale Verzekeringsbank (SVB)

otaal foto's

537 Reacties

2D3D
INTERNAL ANNUAL REPORT:
SOCIALE VERZEKERINGSBANK

ART DIRECTOR:
BILL CAHAN

DESIGNER:
BOB DINETZ

CLIENT:
PROVIDIAN
FINANCIAL

SOFTWARE:
ILLUSTRATOR
PHOTOSHOP
QUARKXPRESS

MATERIALS:
UTOPIA 2 DULL

PRINTING:
LITHOGRAPHIX

CAHAN & ASSOCIATES
PROVIDIAN 2000 ANNUAL REPORT

04

PLEA-SAN-TON, CA

USA

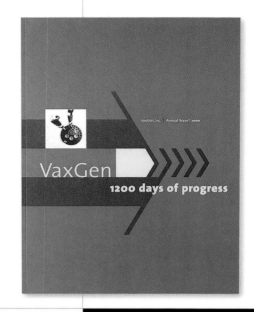

ART DIRECTOR:
ANDREAS KELLER

DESIGNER:
ANDREAS KELLER

PHOTOGRAPHER:
JAMES CHIANG

CLIENT:
VAXGEN, INC

SOFTWARE AND
HARDWARE:
QUARKXPRESS
MAC

MATERIALS:
FRENCH PAPER
SMART WHITE

PRINTING:
ANDERSON
LITHOGRAPH

"After years of working on preclinical studies with animal models, I came to VaxGen because the company is applying all the years of animal research to human testing. That is the only way to determine if a vaccine is effective in preventing infection in people, and the only way we will ever develop a vaccine."

Riri Shibata, D.V.M., Ph.D.
Scientist

"Helping to take VaxGen public in 1999 was a once-in-a-lifetime opportunity. But I am equally gratified by the work we have accomplished in developing the infrastructure for a public company and ensuring that our development projects continue on time and on budget."

Carter Lee, M.B.A.
Senior Vice President
Finance & Administration

"As founder of the International Vaccine Institute, I have seen how important proactive international development campaigns are for vaccines. That's why we're putting so much effort here on working with international agencies such as UNAIDS, the World Health Organization and the World Bank, as well as and private foundations, to plan for the introduction and distribution of AIDSVAX if it proves effective."

Seung-il Shin, Ph.D.
Senior Advisor
International Development

"The success so far of our trials has established us as a leader in AIDS vaccine clinical development. As the first company to conduct Phase III trials for an AIDS vaccine, we realized we had a special responsibility, especially to the volunteers. That's why we designed safety protocols and ethical practices that we believe set a new standard for clinical trials. I think it's a big reason why the trials have progressed so well."

Karin Orelind
Clinical Program Manager

"VaxGen has proved the skeptics wrong at every step. They said you couldn't protect chimps against HIV. We did. They said we'd fail in Phase I and II trials. We didn't. Then they said we'd never be able to enroll the Phase III trials and even if we did we'd have trouble keeping volunteers. Wrong again. But I guess they don't call it conventional wisdom for nothing."

William Heyward, M.D., M.P.H.
Vice President
International Clinical Research

12

13

VINJE DESIGN INC
VAXGEN ANNUAL REPORT 2000

amara holdings limited annual report 2001 **Ascend**

Ascend

SINGAPORE

ART DIRECTORS:
LENG SOH
PANN LIM
ROY POH

DESIGNERS:
LENG SOH
PANN LIM
ROY POH

ILLUSTRATORS:
LENG SOH
PANN LIM
ROY POH

CLIENT:
AMARA SINGAPORE

SOFTWARE AND
HARDWARE:
FREEHAND
PHOTOSHOP
MAC

MATERIALS:
ART PAPER + MAN-
MADE GRASS PATCH

PRINTING:
5CX5C + GLOSS
VARNISH

KINETIC SINGAPORE
ASCEND

ALLEMANN ALMQUIST & JONES
KEYSTONE PROPERTY TRUST
ANNUAL REPORT 2000

ART DIRECTOR:
JAN ALMQUIST

DESIGNER:
ANNE WREN

PHOTOGRAPHER:
CAMERON
DAVIDSON

CLIENT:
KEYSTONE
PROPERTY TRUST

SOFTWARE AND
HARDWARE:
ILLUSTRATOR
PHOTOSHOP
QUARKXPRESS
MAC G4

MATERIALS:
POTLATCH McCOY
GLOSS

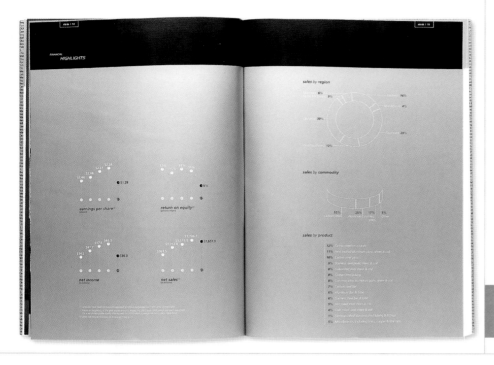

METAL
RS01

ART DIRECTOR:
PEAT JARIYA

DESIGNERS:
PEAT JARIYA
GABE SCHREIBER

CLIENT:
RELIANCE STEEL
& ALU

SOFTWARE AND
HARDWARE:
ILLUSTRATOR
PAGEMAKER
PHOTOSHOP
MAC G4

MATERIALS:
POTLATCH MᶜCOY

PRINTING:
AW

GEE + CHUNG DESIGN
DCM IV Offering Memorandum

ART DIRECTOR:	DESIGNERS:	CLIENT:	TOOLS:	MATERIALS:
Earl Gee	Earl Gee	DCM—Doll Capital	Adobe Photoshop	Stora Enso Centura Dull
	Fani Chung	Management	Adobe InDesign	100 lb (text)

MOVE ME

THE SECRET:

MAKE
YOURSELF
useful.

THE DAVE AND ALEX SHOW

Modem Media View Book

ART DIRECTORS:
Alexander Isley
Dave Goldenber

DESIGNER:
Tracie Rosenkopf-
Lissauer

CLIENT:
Modem Media

TOOLS:
QuarkXPress

MATERIALS:
Monadnock

WE'RE GOING TO DO IT MY WAY

SALTERBAXTER

Boodle Hatfield Corporate Brochure

ART DIRECTOR:	DESIGNER:	CLIENT:	TOOLS:	MATERIALS:
Alan Delgado	Alan Delgado	Boodle Hatfield	QuarkXPress	Rives Reflections (cover)
				Robert Horne Natural (text)

BANDUJO DONKER & BROTHERS

Citigroup Private Bank—Investment Expertise

ART DIRECTOR:	**DESIGNER:**	**CLIENT:**	**TOOLS:**	**MATERIALS:**
Bob Brothers	Laura Astuto	Citigroup Private Bank	Adobe Photoshop QuarkXPress	Mohawk Navajo

BANDUJO DONKER & BROTHERS

Citigroup Private Bank—The Tailored Group

ART DIRECTOR:	DESIGNER:	CLIENT:	TOOLS:	MATERIALS:
Bob Brothers	Laura Astuto	Citigroup Private Bank	Adobe Photoshop QuarkXPress	Mohawk Navajo

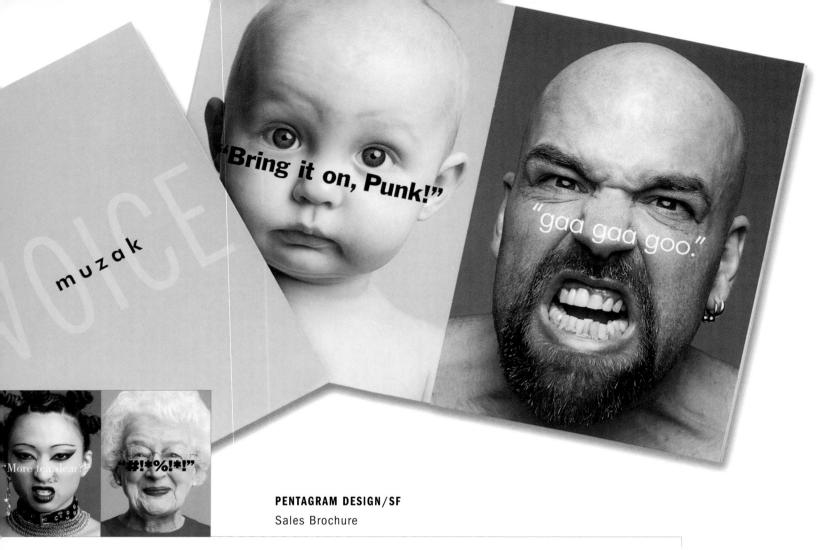

"Bring it on, Punk!"

"gaa gaa goo."

"More tea, dear?"

"#!*%!*!"

PENTAGRAM DESIGN/SF

Sales Brochure

ART DIRECTOR:	DESIGNER:	CLIENT:	TOOLS:
Kit Hinrichs	Laura Scott	Muzak	Adobe Photoshop
			Adobe Illustrator
			QuarkXPress

ZUCCHINI DESIGN PTE LTD

PSB Consulting Marketing Brochure

ART DIRECTOR:	**DESIGNER:**	**CLIENT:**	**TOOLS:**	**MATERIALS:**
Tew Sun Ne	Tew Sun Ne	PSB Corporation	Macromedia Freehand	Translucent PVC 012 mm (cover sleeve) Centuri White 230 gsm (cover) Aspire 130 gsm (text)

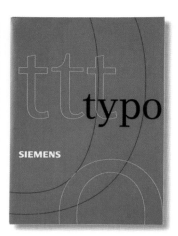

BAUMANN & BAUMANN
Siemens Brand Elements

ART DIRECTORS:	DESIGNERS:	CLIENT:	TOOLS:	MATERIALS:
Barbara and Gerd Baumann	Barbara and Gerd Baumann	Siemens AG Corporate Communications	Adobe InDesign Adobe Photoshop Macromedia Freehand	Phoenix Motion

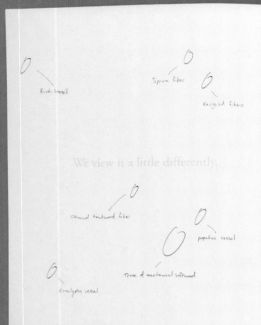

me see this as a cover

So you see, at Econotech Services, we are experts in seeing what others don't. Specifically in the areas of pulping, bleaching, pulp and paper testing, microscopy & wood technology, process chemical analyses and environmental analyses. And since the company was formed in 1972, we've grown to be one of the largest independent pulp and paper testing laboratories in the world.

Accurate, rapid and reliable results are key to our company's substantial expansion, as is the recognized knowledge of our staff. Our initial team of 11 experts has grown to include over 30 research professionals with expertise in chip testing, pulping, bleaching, pulp and paper testing, dissolving pulp evaluation, microscopy, environmental analysis and testing of process samples and liquors. Within a single 19,000 square foot facility, Econotech can perform over 400 analytical tests on everything from wood to finished product, around 100 tests on pulp and paper products and over 50 different microscopy tests.

Econotech's international clientele includes pulp and paper mills, equipment suppliers, chemical suppliers, consulting engineers and universities. In addition to providing unbiased, independent and confidential evaluations of new processes or chemicals, Econotech assists clients in the development of new equipment, the design of new mills and the evaluation of chemical costs involved in mill modernization. >>

HANGAR 18 CREATIVE GROUP
Econotech Brochure

DESIGNER:
Kim Wolf

CLIENT:
Econotech Services

TOOLS:
QuarkXPress

MATERIALS:
Cougar Opaque
(text and cover)

04. MICROSCOPY AND WOOD TECHNOLOGY

OBJECTIVE TURRET ON OPTICAL MICROSCOPE

Microscopy is an indispensable testing discipline for the pulp and paper industry. The primary application is fiber analysis, which provides detailed evaluations of wood species and pulp type in paper, pulp and wood samples.

Contaminant identification is also a large portion of the work we do in the Microscopy Department. This provides valuable assistance in process troubleshooting. In addition to light microscopic techniques, we have access to scanning electron microscopy and Fourier Transform infra-red analysis. Digital photomicrographs enhance reports and provide instant visualization of contaminants and defects.

Microscopy is an art as much as a science and requires many years of training and experience to become proficient. The Microscopy Group has over 30 years combined experience in analyzing the untold variety of samples that are submitted. We have extensive reference resources including natural and man-made fibers, particle and contaminant samples and permanent slides. >>

HALLMARK LOYALTY

How to Stand Out in the Crowd: Profiting from Personalization

ART DIRECTOR:
Christopher Huelshorst

DESIGNER:
Christine Taylor

EDITORIAL DIRECTOR:
Stacey Hsu

COPYWRITER:
Janet Walnik

PHOTOGRAPHY:
Ambrosi & Associates,
Chicago

PRINTER:
Nies Artcraft, St. Louis

CLIENT:
State Farm

TOOLS:
QuarkXPress

MATERIALS:
Mohawk Superfine

DIRECTIONS#3
TRENDS IN CSR REPORTING 2002-03
A JOINT REPORT BY SALTERBAXTER & CONTEXT

context salterbaxter

SALTERBAXTER

Directions 3 Report

ART DIRECTOR:	DESIGNER:	CLIENT:	TOOLS:	MATERIALS:
Alan Delgado	Alan Delgado	Salterbaxter	QuarkXPress	Flockage cover

WEYMOUTH DESIGN

Sappi 2002 Annual Report Show

ART DIRECTOR:	DESIGNERS:	CLIENT:	TOOLS:	MATERIALS:
Tom Laidlaw	Robert Krivicich	Sappi Fine Paper	QuarkXPress	Sappi Fine Paper
	Brad Lewthwaite	North America	Adobe Photoshop	

CURRENTLY
THERE IS NO FDA APPROVED
MEDICAL TREATMENT WHICH
CREATES A SIGNIFICANT MEDICAL
AND MARKET OPPORTUNITY.

SEX
HAS BEEN PROVEN TO BE GOOD
FOR YOUR HEALTH.

VIVUS 03

HOWRY DESIGN ASSOCIATES

Viuus 2003 Annual Report

ART DIRECTOR:	DESIGNER:	CLIENT:	TOOLS:	MATERIALS:
Jill Howry	Ty Whittington	Vivus Inc	Adobe Photoshop QuarkXPress	Utopia II matte 80 lb

ED
(ERECTILE DYSFUNCTION)
IS THE INABILITY TO ACHIEVE OR
SUSTAIN AN ERECTION ADEQUATE
FOR SATISFYING SEXUAL ACTIVITY.

Work

Team

"For ABX EGF we opted
for an IgG₁ subclass,
and the challenge was to
come up with an antibody
that had suitable affinity and
suitable selectivity for the
cell-surface EGF receptor,
so that it would have
potential as a therapeutic.
That antibody
is now in clinical trials."

Just another day in bioscience.

And just another challenge
for Millipore. We help our customers
shrink discovery time, simplify
development processes, optimize the
manufacturing of biotherapeutics,
and leap regulatory hurdles
by making it all pure, pure, pure.

WEYMOUTH DESIGN
Millipore AR 2003

ART DIRECTOR:	DESIGNER:	WRITER:	PHOTOGRAPHER:	TOOLS:	MATERIALS:
Michael Weymouth	Bob Kellerman	Tom Anderson	Michael Weymouth	Adobe Photoshop Adobe Illustrator QuarkXPress	100 lb Sappi McCoy matte (cover) 100 lb Sappi McCoy matte (text)

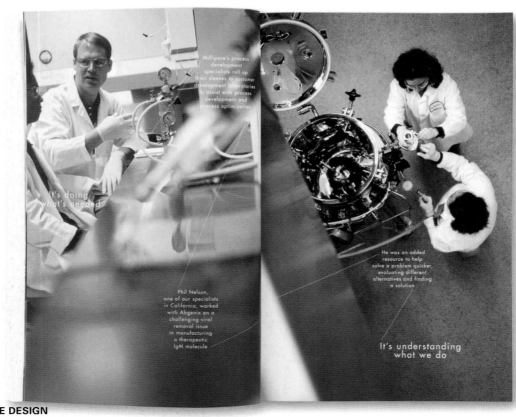

Millipore's process
development
specialists roll up
their sleeves in customer
development laboratories
to assist with process
development and
process optimization.

It's doing
what's needed

Phil Nelson,
one of our specialists
in California, worked
with Abgenix on a
challenging viral
removal issue
in manufacturing
a therapeutic
IgM molecule.

He was an added
resource to help
solve a problem quicker,
evaluating different
alternatives and finding
a solution.

It's understanding
what we do

SALTERBAXTER

British Library Annual Report 2002-2003

ART DIRECTOR:
Penny Baxter

DESIGNER:
Hannah Griffiths

CLIENT:
British Library

TOOLS:
QuarkXPress

MATERIALS:
Hello Silk 150 gsm (text)
Arjo Wiggins
"Impressions Design"
300 gsm (cover)

MONSTER DESIGN

Unitus Annual Report

ART DIRECTORS:
Theresa Monica
Hannah Wygal

DESIGNER:
Madeleine Eiche

CLIENT:
Unitus

TOOLS:
Adobe Photoshop
Macromedia Freehand
QuarkXPress

IMELDA AGENCY

Corporate Annual Report

Art Director:
Urukalo Saso

Designer:
Urukalo Saso

Client:
Energetika Ljublyana

Materials:
on offset

POPCORN INITIATIVE

KUA 2003 Annual Report—ON

ART DIRECTOR:
Chris Jones

DESIGNERS:
Chris Jones
Roger Wood

CLIENT:
Chris Gent, Kissimmee
Utility Authority

TOOLS:
Adobe InDesign
Adobe Illustrator

MATERIALS:
Fox River
Coronado SST
Stipple 80 lb (cover)
formed rubber

HORNALL ANDERSON DESIGN WORKS, INC.

Tree Top 2003 Annual Report

ART DIRECTOR:	DESIGNERS:	CLIENT:	TOOLS:	MATERIALS:
Katha Dalton	Katha Dalton	Tree Top	Adobe Photoshop	Mohawk 100 lb
	Tiffany Place		QuarkXPress	Superfine Text Smooth
	John Anderle			Ultrawhite (text)
	Beckon Wyld			Mohawk 80 lb Superfine
				Text Smooth Ultrawhite
				(inserts)
				Mohawk 100 lb
				Superfine Cover Smooth
				Ultrawhite (cover)

WEYMOUTH DESIGN

Courier 2003 Annual Report

ART DIRECTOR:	DESIGNER:	CLIENT:	TOOLS:	MATERIALS:
Robert Krivicich	Aaron Haesaert	Courier Corporation	Adobe Photoshop Adobe Illustrator QuarkXPress	Sappi McCoy, Finch Opaque

pay attention
to shareholders

$2.5M

Every dog counts.

THE CHASE
**Manchester Dogs'
Home**

Art Director:
Harriet Devoy
Designer:
Steve Royle
Client:
Manchester Dogs'
Home
Software:
QuarkXPress,
Adobe Illustrator,
Adobe Photoshop
Paper/Materials:
Neptune Unique

6,796 dogs

Manchester Dogs' Home Annual Review 2001-2002

were admitted to
Manchester Dogs'
Home last year.
So where do they
all come from?

9 out of 10 dogs were happily rehomed. That's 5,947 in total.

What have we achieved this year?

MESSAGE FROM THE PRESIDENT

When I sit down with my son and talk about his career plans, or how he views world issues, or... just life, I'm struck by the mind-boggling pace and extent of social change. The world his generation is growing up in is utterly unpredictable. Its distinguishing feature is an incredibly complicated environment of choice. Choice that is more promising, yet more forbidding, than anything my generation faced. What if you could genetically alter your unborn child? What if you had to undergo an eye scan each time you visited a bank, voted, or applied for insurance? What if the world had a CEO? And countries had no borders? These are questions confronted by no previous generation.

18 – 19

IRIDIUM, A DESIGN AGENCY/KOLEGRAM
SSHRC
Annual Report

Art Directors:
Jean-Luc Denat,
Mario L'Écuyer
Designers:
Mario L'Écuyer,
David Daigle
Client:
SSHRC
Software:
QuarkXPress,
Adobe Illustrator,
Adobe Photoshop
Paper/Materials:
Sappi Lustro Dull,
Domtar Cornwall
Pinweave, Rolland
Opaque Smooth

PRODUCT
AND SERVICE
BROCHURES

d create

DESIGN FIRM > Kesselskramer
ART DIRECTOR > Erik Kessels
DESIGNER > Karen Heuter
ILLUSTRATORS/PHOTOGRAPHERS > Stang, Bianca Pilet
COPYWRITER > David Bell
CLIENT > Do
TOOLS (SOFTWARE/PLATFORM) > QuarkXPress, Apple Macintosh
PAPER STOCK/PRINTING PROCESS > Cyclus print
PRINTING PROCESS > Offset, sheet

DESIGN FIRM > Zappata Diseñadores S.C.
ART DIRECTOR > Ibo Angulo
DESIGNER > Ibo Angulo
PHOTOGRAPHER > Ricardo Trabulsi
CLIENT > Laura Lavalle
TOOLS (SOFTWARE/PLATFORM) > Photoshop, Freehand
PRINTING PROCESS > Offset

DESIGN FIRM › Zappata Diseñadores S.C.
ART DIRECTOR › Ibo Angulo
DESIGNER › Ibo Angulo
COPYWRITER › © Disney/Pixar
CLIENT › Cupa Chups
TOOLS (SOFTWARE/PLATFORM) › Adobe Illustrator
PRINTING PROCESS › Offset

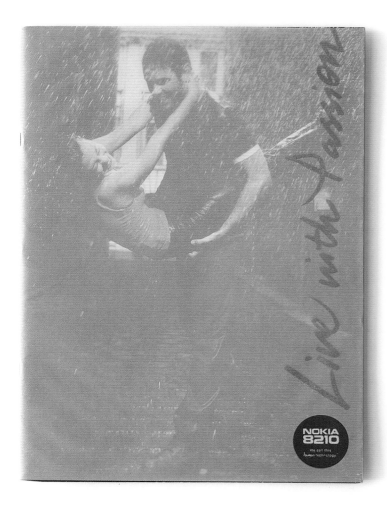

DESIGN FIRM › 141 Singapore Pte Ltd.
ART DIRECTOR › Winnie Lee
DESIGNER › Wnnie Lee
ILLUSTRATORS/PHOTOGRAPHERS › Tomek and Eryk Photography Pty
COPYWRITER › Kok Chin Yin
CLIENT › Nokia Pte Ltd.
PAPER STOCK › Cover—112gsm GSK transparent paper; text—210 gsm Eagle Silhouette matt artcard
PRINTING PROCESS › Cover—3c x 0c; text—5c x 5c, solid matt artcard

DESIGN FIRM > Palmquist Creative
ART DIRECTORS > Kurt Palmquist, Kelly Bellcour
DESIGNERS > Kurt Palmquist, Kelly Bellcour
PHOTOGRAPHERS > Rob Wilke, Denver Bryan
COPYWRITER > Client
CLIENT > Field & Stream
TOOLS (SOFTWARE/PLATFORM) > Adobe Pagemaker, Illustrator, Macintosh
PAPER STOCK/PRINTING PROCESS > Frostbrite, 80 lb. book, white

DESIGN FIRM > Alternatives
ART DIRECTOR > Julie Koch-Beinke
DESIGNER > Julie Koch-Beinke
ILLUSTRATOR/PHOTOGRAPHER > Various
CLIENT > Sungold Eyewear
TOOLS (SOFTWARE/PLATFORM) > Illustrator, Macintosh
PAPER STOCK > Metallic pearl white for cover, 100 lb. gloss cover
PRINTING PROCESS > Four-color process

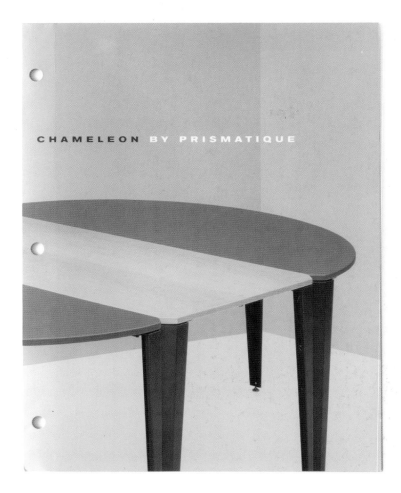

CHAMELEON BY PRISMATIQUE

DESIGN FIRM › Dinnick & Howells
ART DIRECTOR › Jonathan Howells
DESIGNERS › Dwayne Dobson, Tracey Hanson
CLIENT › Prismatique
TOOLS (SOFTWARE/PLATFORM) › Macintosh G3, Illustrator, Photoshop

DESIGN FIRM › Sibley Peteet Design
ART DIRECTOR › Don Sibley
DESIGNERS › Don Sibley, Donna Aldridge
PHOTOGRAPHERS › Various
COPYWRITER › Don Sibley
CLIENT › Weyerhaeuser Paper
TOOLS (SOFTWARE/PLATFORM) › QuarkXPress, Macintosh
PAPER STOCK › Weyerhaeuser Cougar opaque

DESIGN FIRM › Creative Conspiracy, Inc.

ART DIRECTOR › Kris Hickcox

DESIGNER › Kris Hickcox

ILLUSTRATOR/PHOTOGRAPHER › Neil Hannum

CLIENT › Screaming Rhino Gift Market

TOOLS (SOFTWARE/PLATFORM) › QuarkXPress, Illustrator, Photoshop

PAPER STOCK/PRINTING PROCESS › Catalog: 80 lb. McCoy—text; 4/4 with bleeds—cover.
Env: 80 lb. Gilbert Voice in Rye

DESIGN FIRM > Arias Associates
ART DIRECTOR > Mauricio Arias
DESIGNER > Mauricio Arias
ILLUSTRATORS/PHOTOGRAPHERS > Mike Halbert, Stefano Massei
COPYWRITER > Pottery Barn
CLIENT > Pottery Barn
TOOLS (SOFTWARE/PLATFORM) > QuarkXPress, Photoshop
PAPER STOCK > Champion Benefit, Mohawk superfine
PRINTING PROCESS > Lithography and letterpress

DESIGN FIRM > Giorgio Rocco Communications
ART DIRECTOR > Giorgio Rocco
DESIGNER > Giorgio Rocco
ILLUSTRATOR/PHOTOGRAPHER > Archives INDA
COPYWRITER > Elisabetta Campo
CLIENT > INDA spa, Italy
TOOLS (SOFTWARE/PLATFORM) > Macintosh, Photoshop, Freehand
PAPER STOCK > Burgo
PRINTING PROCESS > Four-color offset

DESIGN FIRM > Kan & Lau Design Consultants
ART DIRECTORS > Kan Tai-keung, Veronica Cheung, Mak Tsing Kuoh
DESIGNERS > Kan Tai-keung, Veronica Cheung, Mak Tsing Kuoh
COMPUTER ILLUSTRATOR > Ng Cheuk Bong
CLIENT > Rolex (HK) Ltd

DESIGN FIRM › Hand Made Group
ART DIRECTORS › Alessandro Esteri, Giona Maisrelli
DESIGNERS › Alessandro Esteri, Giona Maisrelli
ILLUSTRATOR/PHOTOGRAPHER › Alessandro Esteri
COPYWRITER › Verdiana Maggiorelli
CLIENT › Marco Pierguidi
TOOLS (SOFTWARE/PLATFORM) › QuarkXPress, Photoshop
PAPER STOCK › Garda
PRINTING PROCESS › Four-color

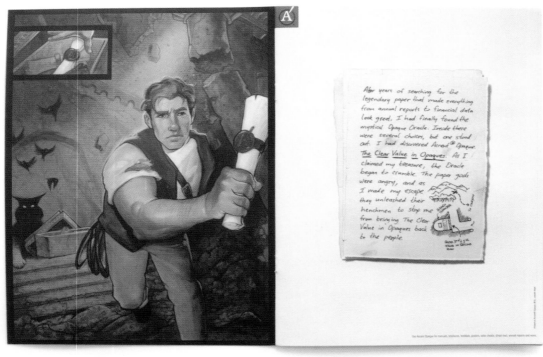

DESIGN FIRM > Oden Marketing and Design
CREATIVE DIRECTOR > Bret Terwilleger
DESIGNER > Michael Guthrie
ILLUSTRATOR > Michael Koelsch
PENCILS > Dean Zachary
COPYWRITER > Henry Ellis
CLIENT > Accent Opaque
PAPER STOCK > Williamson

Vegetables are always
on our mind.

DESIGN FIRM > Lorenz Advertising
ART DIRECTOR > Glen Miranda
DESIGNER > Glen Miranda
ILLUSTRATORS/PHOTOGRAPHERS > Dan Thoner, various photographers
COPYWRITER > Carm Greco
CLIENT > Enza Zaden North America
TOOLS (SOFTWARE/PLATFORM) > QuarkXPress, Photoshop, Macintosh
PAPER STOCK > Simpson evergreen cord
PRINTING PROCESS > Five-color lithography

INTRODUCTION • HISTORY

We've come a long way in this business...
all the way from Holland.

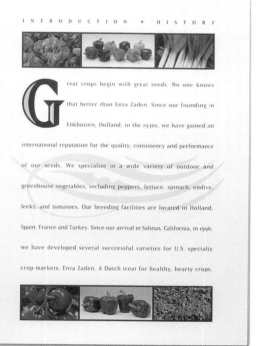

INTRODUCTION • HISTORY

Great crops begin with great seeds. No one knows that better than Enza Zaden. Since our founding in Enkhuizen, Holland, in the 1930s, we have gained an international reputation for the quality, consistency and performance of our seeds. We specialize in a wide variety of outdoor and greenhouse vegetables, including peppers, lettuce, spinach, endive, leeks, and tomatoes. Our breeding facilities are located in Holland, Spain, France and Turkey. Since our arrival in Salinas, California, in 1996, we have developed several successful varieties for U.S. specialty crop markets. Enza Zaden. A Dutch treat for healthy, hearty crops.

DESIGNFIRM > Lee Reedy Creative
ART DIRECTOR > Lee Reedy
DESIGNER > Heather Haworth
ILLUSTRATORS/PHOTOGRAPHERS > Bruce Wolf, Marshal Safron, Michael Peck
COPYWRITER > Carol Parsons
CLIENT > Hunter Douglas
TOOLS (SOFTWARE/PLATFORM) > QuarkXPress
PAPER STOCK > McCoy, laminated and U.V. coated

DESIGN FIRM > Tycoon Graphics
ART DIRECTOR > Tycoon Graphics
DESIGNER > Tycoon Graphics
PHOTOGRAPHER > Shoji Uchida
CLIENT > Abahouse International Co., Ltd.

DESIGN FIRM › Clarity Coverdale Fury
ART DIRECTOR › Jac Coverdale
DESIGNER › Jac Coverdale
ILLUSTRATORS › Bill Cook, Peter Sjn, Kate Thomessen, Time Life Books
PHOTOGRAPHER › Raymond Meeks
COPYWRITER › Jerry Fury
CLIENT › Millennium Import Co.
TOOLS (SOFTWARE/PLATFORM) › Illustrator, QuarkXPress, Photoshop, Macintosh
PAPER STOCK › Cover: 130 lb. Curtis back linen; text: 80 lb. Cougar natural smooth
PRINTING PROCESS › Cover: foil stamped, two-colors; text: offset, six-colors, two sides

NAAM: THEO VERGEER · CLUB: DE GRAAFSCHAP · MERK: MIELE EXPERT · WASMIDDEL: WEISHEER · HOOFDPUNT: BRAND WORDS KORTSLUITING IN DE EXPERT · TEMPERATUUR: 40 GRADEN · INS GROOTHANDEL

NAAM: JOHANNA KRUIZE · CLUB: PSV · MERK: WHIRLPOOL (VIA PHILIPS) · MOTTO: GRASVLEKKEN ZET JE IN DE WEEK · WASMIDDEL: ALL · TEMPERATUUR: 40 GRADEN

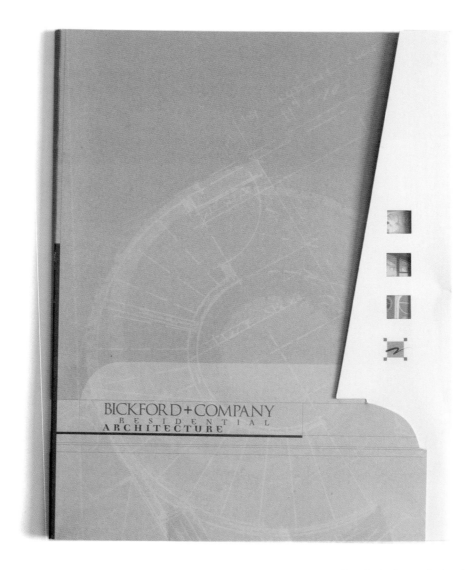

DESIGN FIRM > Tracy Design Communications, Inc.
ART DIRECTOR > Jan Tracy
DESIGNER > Anthony Magliano
ILLUSTRATORS/PHOTOGRAPHERS > Miscellaneous
COPYWRITER > Robin Zaplin
CLIENT > Bickford & Co.
TOOLS (SOFTWARE/PLATFORM) > QuarkXPress, Photoshop

DESIGN FIRM > IE Design
ART DIRECTOR > Marcie Carson
DESIGNER > Marcie Carson
CLIENT > Kern & Wooley LLP
TOOLS (SOFTWARE/PLATFORM) > Macintosh, Illustrator, Photoshop, QuarkXPress
PAPER STOCK/PRINTING PROCESS > Cover: Havana Structeras-Perla; text: Gilbert Oxford Cream
PRINTING PROCESS > Cover: two-color PMJS

SOLUTIONS

OSBORN
MALEDON

www.osbornmaledon.com

DESIGN FIRM > After Hours Creative
ART DIRECTOR > After Hours Creative
DESIGNER > After Hours Creative
COPYWRITER > After Hours Creative
CLIENT > Osborn Maledon
TOOLS (SOFTWARE/PLATFORM) > Macintosh G4, Illustrator

COMPLEX

The best lawyers solve complicated problems in ways their clients can understand. • Osborn Maledon attorneys have the judgment, knowledge and experience to bring clarity to complex situations. You receive no-nonsense solutions to difficult business issues, from challenging litigation to mergers, acquisitions and public offerings. We know what it takes to get business done. And what it takes to help you achieve your goals. If everything were simple, your choice of a law firm wouldn't matter. When things get complicated, Osborn Maledon offers a clear solution.

CREATIVE

By moving just one glass, arrange the top row to look like the bottom row.

Hydrothermal massage tubs in every room. A full range of spa services. The finest comforts and amenities refresh the spirit.

DESIGN FIRM > Arias Associates
ART DIRECTORS > Mauricio Arias, Maral Sarkis
DESIGNERS > Mauricio Arias, Maral Sarkis
COPYWRITER > Dawn Mortensen
CLIENT > Hotel Casa Del Mar
TOOLS (SOFTWARE/PLATFORM) > QuarkXPress, Photoshop, Illustrator
PAPER STOCK > Mohawk superfine and McCoy silk
PRINTING PROCESS > Lithography, embossing and letterpress

DESIGN FIRM > Arias Associates
ART DIRECTORS > Mauricio Arias, Maral Sarkis, Steve Mortensen, Stephanie Yee
DESIGNERS > Mauricio Arias, Maral Sarkis, Steve Mortensen, Stephanie Yee
ILLUSTRATOR/PHOTOGRAPHER > Fred Licht
COPYWRITER > Words by Design
CLIENT > Crescent Heights
TOOLS (SOFTWARE/PLATFORM) > QuarkXPress, Photoshop, Illustrator
PAPER STOCK > Starwhite Vicksburg
PRINTING PROCESS > Lithography, letterpress

"two voices are there: one is of the sea, one of the mountains; each a mighty voice."

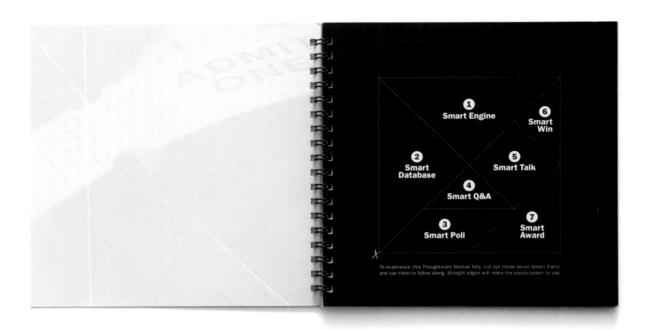

Anatomy of a *SmartSpiff*

When your Thoughtware calls for a *SmartSpiff* certificate, entry ticket or game piece, you can choose from many distinct constructions, shapes, sizes and materials. Design your *SmartSpiff* to adhere to your packaging with security features, or seal it in food barrier wrap for insertion with your product, or include a multi-fold brochure in your construction, or die cut a shape relating to your campaign's theme — virtually *anything* is possible.

The most cost-efficient construction is a two-ply, dry-seal rectangular format that peels apart and yields four copy panels. At right is an example shown at actual size.

10

DESIGN FIRM > Aspen Interactive
ART DIRECTOR > Ken Weightman
DESIGNER > Ken Weightman
CLIENT > Phoneworks
TOOLS (SOFTWARE/PLATFORM) > QuarkXPress, Adobe Photoshop, Macintosh
PAPER STOCK/PRINTING PROCESS > Four-color process and one match color

DESIGN FIRM > Sayles Graphic Design
ART DIRECTOR > John Sayles
DESIGNER > John Sayles
PHOTOGRAPHERS > David Crosby, Tony Smith
ILLUSTRATOR > John Sayles
COPYWRITER > Wendy Lyons
CLIENT > Greenville South Carolina Convention & Visitors Bureau
TOOLS (SOFTWARE/PLATFORM) > QuarkXPress, Macintosh
PRINTING PROCESS > Offset printed, includes tipped-on samples

perfect aim

perfect fit

DESIGN FIRM > Sibley Peteet Design
ART DIRECTOR > Donna Aldridge
DESIGNER > Donna Aldridge
ILLUSTRATOR > Brandon Kirk
COPYWRITER > Don Sibley
CLIENT > Williamson Printing Company
TOOLS (SOFTWARE/PLATFORM) > QuarkXPress, Macintosh
PAPER STOCK > Strobe

DESIGN FIRM > Erbe Design
ART DIRECTOR > Maureen Erbe
DESIGNER > Maureen Erbe
ILLUSTRATOR > Allison Starcher
COPYWRITER > Maureen Gilmer
CLIENT > Monrovia
TOOLS (SOFTWARE/PLATFORM) > QuarkXPress
PRINTING PROCESS > Lithography

DESIGN FIRM > Hornall Anderson Design Works, Inc.
ART DIRECTOR > Jack Anderson
DESIGNERS > Jack Anderson, Belinda Bowling, Andrew Smith, Ed Lee
ILLUSTRATOR > Jack Unruh
COPYWRITERS > Various
CLIENT > Streamworks
TOOLS (SOFTWARE/PLATFORM) > QuarkXPress, Photoshop
PAPER STOCK > French Speckletone Kraft cover, natural text

DESIGN FIRM > Lee Reedy Creative
ART DIRECTOR > Lee Reedy
DESIGNER > Lee Reedy
ILLUSTRATOR/PHOTOGRAPHER > Stock
COPYWRITER > Suzy Patterson
CLIENT > Travel Connections
TOOLS (SOFTWARE/PLATFORM) > QuarkXPress
PAPER STOCK > Chipboard
PRINTING PROCESS > Two-color

KO CRÉATION
S BY SHAN: COLLECTION 2002

ART DIRECTOR:	DESIGNERS:	PHOTOGRAPHER:	CLIENT:	SOFTWARE:
POL BARIL	ANNIE LACHAPELLE	JOËL DUMOULIN	SHAN	PHOTOSHOP
	POL BARIL			QUARKXPRESS

USINE DE BOUTONS
PIRELLI/DUCATI DFX RACING TEAM

ART DIRECTORS:	DESIGNER:	CLIENT:	PRINTING:
LIONELLO BOREAN	LIONELLO BOREAN	PIRELLI/DUCATI DFX	CMYK + GOLD
CHIARA GRANDESSO	CHIARA GRANDESSO	RACING TEAM	

ITALY

MADE THOUGHT
SONNETI SPRING/SUMMER 2002
LOOK BOOK

ART DIRECTORS:
BEN PARKER
PAUL AUSTIN

DESIGNERS:
BEN PARKER
PAUL AUSTIN

PHOTOGRAPHER:
GEMMA BOOTH

CLIENT:
SONNETI

PRINTING:
PERIVAN

New Fiction

Going Out
Scarlett Thomas

FROST DESIGN
FOURTH ESTATE CATALOG 2002

ART DIRECTOR:
VINCE FROST

DESIGNER:
VINCE FROST

ILLUSTRATOR:
MARION DEUCHARS

CLIENT:
FOURTH ESTATE

MATERIALS:
PAPER EPSILON
NERO BY FENNER
PAPER120GSM +
270GSM

PRINTING:
SCREEN PRINTING
BY LAUREN
DISPLAYS

HEBE. WERBUNG & DESIGN
MAAS PRODUCT FOLDER

ART DIRECTOR:
REINER HEBE

DESIGNER:
STEFANIE WAHL

ILLUSTRATOR:
DOMINIK ZEHLE

CLIENT:
MAAS GOLDSMITH,
STUTTGART

SOFTWARE AND
HARDWARE:
QUARKXPRESS
MAC

THE KITCHEN
DAY/NIGHT

UK

ART DIRECTORS:
ROB PETRIE
PHIL SIMS

What appears to be is what I deal with.

sn

Sometimes, hum... the scene you p... take a picture of... and it's lifeless, ... you can take a pi... scratching his n... great picture. □ I am a professional photographer by trade and an amateur photographer by vocation. Most of the time when I am out of the house I carry a small unobtrusive camera and I snap away obsessively at things that interest me and whatever I think would make a good picture.

USA
█ EMERSON, WAJDOWICZ STUDIOS
BRAVO ERWITT

museums

I go to museums to people watch. Because everyone there has gone to look and they are captured in a concentrated place, it is a particularly good thing. For a photographer, rather than fly casting, it's like shooting fish in a barrel. □ It is amazing how something which isn't much of anything becomes important when it's framed. Often the frames are more artistic than their contents. They are very reassuring, like the labels. Some people spend more time looking at the labels than at the work itself.

In the end all museums are interesting. Even when they're not.

ART DIRECTORS:	DESIGNERS:	CLIENT:	SOFTWARE:	MATERIALS:	PRINTING:
JUREK WAJDOWICZ	JUREK WAJDOWICZ	DOMTAR	QUARKXPRESS	BRAVO	MACDONALD
LISA LAROCHELLE	LISA LAROCHELLE				PRINTING
	MANNY MENDEZ				

If my pictures help some people to see things in a certain way, it's probably to look

at serious things non-seriously. Everything's serious. Everything's not serious.

PRODUCT AND SERVICE BROCHURES 115

C375
KREABAGNO BROCHURE

ROMA | *Arte*

Oval biçimli köşe duş tekneleri için tasarlanmış, 2 dışa açılır kapı ve 2 sabit panelden oluşan duş kabini.
Rounded shower enclosure with two pivot doors and two fixed panels for corner shower trays.

ART DIRECTOR:	DESIGNER:	PHOTOGRAPHERS:	CLIENT:	SOFTWARE:	MATERIALS:	PRINTING:
CEM ERUTKU	SEMA DEMIRCIFT	BULENT ERUTKU EMRE IKIZLER	KREABAGNO	FREEHAND PHOTOSHOP	MODO	4-COLOR OFFSET

SIENA | *Arte*

ART DIRECTOR:
KIT HINRICHS

DESIGNER:
MARIA WENZEL

CLIENT:
POTLATCH PAPER

SOFTWARE AND
HARDWARE:
ILLUSTRATOR
PHOTOSHOP
MAC

MATERIALS:
POTLATCH

PRINTING:
ANDERSON,
LOS ANGELES

PENTAGRAM SF
MCCOY REUNION

USA

THE KITCHEN
NO BOOK

UK

Q
MISSION STRATAKOLOUR

ART DIRECTOR:
THILO VON
DEBSCHITZ

DESIGNER:
MATTHIAS FREY

PHOTOGRAPHER:
MATTHIAS FREY

CLIENT:
ARJO WIGGINS
GERMANY

SOFTWARE AND
HARDWARE:
ILLUSTRATOR
QUARKXPRESS
MAC

MATERIALS:
STRATAKOLOUR

PRINTING:
GORIUS DRUCK &
SERVICE

ART DIRECTOR:	DESIGNER:	CLIENT:	SOFTWARE AND	MATERIALS:	PRINTING:
ANN WILLOUGHBY	TRENTON KENAGY	EL DORADO INC	HARDWARE:	UNCOATED	IN-HOUSE
			QUARKXPRESS	CHIPBOARD	
			MAC		

USA

WILLOUGHBY DESIGN GROUP
BARN BOOK

SINNBILD UND MASSSTAB FÜR FEINSTES WOHNEN.

HARVESTEHUDE

ART DIRECTORS:
MARIUS FAHRNER
UMUB ETTERLIG

DESIGNERS:
MARIUS FAHRNER
UMUB ETTERLIG

CLIENT:
DAHLER & COMPANY
PROJECT MARKETING

SOFTWARE:
FREEHAND

MATERIALS:
RÖMERTURM
CURTIS ESPARTO

PRINTING:
4-COLOR OFFSET

MARIUS FAHRNER DESIGN
AVANTGARDE

GERMANY

ROSE DESIGN ASSOCIATES, LTD
WESTZONE AUTUMN CATALOG

Afghanistan
Chris Steele-Perkins

The ageless rhythms of daily life
in Afghanistan's fields, villages
and towns are disrupted by war,
displacement and natural disaster.

UK/US/Can	Publication	UK Format	US Format	Page extent	Photographs	Cover	ISBN
£30/$50/$75	Published	313 x 235mm	9¼ x 12¼"	128pp	76 duotone	Hardcover	1 903391 13 X

Stones: The Megaliths of
England & Wales and the
Stories Behind Them
David and Lai Ngan Corio

Stunning photography is accompanied
by the fascinating variety of literature,
opinions and fantasies inspired by the
presence of ancient stones on the
British landscape.

UK/US/Can	Publication	UK Format	US Format	Page extent	Photographs	Cover	ISBN
£30/$50/$75	Published	254 x 254mm	10 x 10"	160pp	64 duotone	Hardcover	1 903391 15 6

The Divine Frenzy:
Ritual and Possession
in Hindu Kerala
Pepita Seth

Illuminating photographs and texts
chart the way in which the people
of this region of southern India fuse
with their land and their gods.

UK/US/Can	Publication	UK Format	US Format	Page extent	Photographs	Cover	ISBN
£30/$55/$75	Published	300 x 245mm	9½ x 12"	208pp	140 colour	Hardcover	1 903391 14 8

Carving the Mountains:
The Marble Quarries of Carrara
Guido Buffoni and Stephen Cox

Guido Buffoni has photographed
the marble quarries of northern
Italy since the 1970s. His images
are accompanied by an overview
of Carrara's history by British
sculptor Stephen Cox.

UK/US/Can	Publication	UK Format	US Format	Page extent	Photographs	Cover	ISBN
£40/$85/$100	April 2001	300 x 300mm	12 x 12"	192pp	120 colour + b/w	Hardcover	1 903391 22 9

Fuck Off Typography
Various
Edited by Gerard Saint

Rush
*Jocelyn Bain Hogg
and Neil Rollinson*

Londoners love and hate their home in equal measure. Not that they would demonstrate such strong emotions in public – such things are best left to the hot-heads of New York, Paris or Rome. Instead they set their city faces hard and walk apart, though with the herd. Occasionally they will let their hair down – at New Year's Eve, for example. Momentarily, they may give vent to their frustration at missing a bus or losing a purse. But before long it's back to the routine, as if nothing ever happened, dreaming personal island dreams as the herd returns to graze.

Photographer Jocelyn Bain Hogg has teamed up with award-winning poet Neil Rollinson to explore the 21st-century London experience, from the remnants of Empire to 'Cool Britannia' chic, from the chaos of a groaning public transport system to moments of tranquility in the city's parks and gardens.

Author
Jocelyn Bain Hogg's last book, *The Firm*, a study of Britain's criminal underworld, was published by Westzone in February 2001 and was featured in the Sunday Times magazine. His other photographic credits include *Time Out*, *GQ*, *Esquire*, *Mixx*, *The Face* and *Vanity Fair*.

Neil Rollinson is a past winner of the National Poetry Competition and the author of the critically acclaimed collection *A Spillage of Mercury*. His poetry is observant, astute, irreverent and witty, offering entertaining insights into contemporary city life.

For further information
call +44 (0)20 7734 6002

westzone®
now available on line

preview© Autumn 2001

ART DIRECTOR:
SIMON ELLIOTT

DESIGNER:
SIMON ELLIOTT

CLIENT:
WESTZONE
PUBLISHING, LTD

SOFTWARE:
ILLUSTRATOR
PHOTOSHOP
QUARKXPRESS

MATERIALS:
VALLIANT SATIN ART

PRINTING:
OFFSET LITHO

Fuck Off Typography
Various
Edited by Gerard Saint

Publication
June

Cover price
£40

Format
330mm x 265mm

Page extent
176

Illustrations
124 colour +
b/w plates

Cover
Hardcover

ISBN
1 903391 21 0

Title
Fuck Off Typography invites prolific typographers, graphic designers and illustrators from the UK and international scene to trade visual insults. Peppered with expletives, *Fuck Off Typography* explores and offers insight into obscure taboo colloquialisms, and explores the creation of brand new, sharp-witted profanities expressed through the medium of typography.

Contributors include Paul Davis, Jasper Goodall, Dave Foldvari, Michael Gillette, Christophe Gowans, London design companies Form, Monster and many others, alongside their illustrious international contemporaries.

Author
Gerard Saint is an art director and co-founder of the London design group Big-Active.

FABIO ONGARATO DESIGN
EXPRESSION PAPER PROMO

AUSTRALIA

ART DIRECTOR:	DESIGNER:	PHOTOGRAPHER:	CLIENT:	MATERIALS:	PRINTING:
FABIO ONGARATO	YARRA LAURIE	DEREK HENDERSON	K. W. DOGGETT	EXPRESSION	GUNN & TAYLOR

ART DIRECTOR:
JOHANNES PLASS

DESIGNER:
KRISTINA
DULLMANN

PHOTOGRAPHER:
CARSTEN RAFFEL

CLIENT:
SINNER SCHRADER

MATERIALS:
ZANDERS MEDLEY
PURE

PRINTING:
DRUCKGEREI
BRÜNNER

MUTABOR DESIGN
SINNER SCHRADER RECRUITING FLYER

GERMANY

AJANS ULTRA
VAKKO SUPREFINE/
CHOCOLATTE BOOK

ART DIRECTOR:	DESIGNER:	PHOTOGRAPHER:	CLIENT:	SOFTWARE:	MATERIALS:	PRINTING:
NAZLI ONGAN	NAZLI ONGAN	ABDULLAH HEKIMHAN	VAKKO	FREEHAND	NONBRILLIANT GLAZED PAPER	4-COLOR OFFSET

ART DIRECTOR:
MARTIN STILLHART

DESIGNER:
MARTIN STILLHART

CLIENT:
SKIM.COM

SOFTWARE:
ILLUSTRATOR
QUARKXPRESS

MATERIALS:
INVERCOAT 240GSM

PRINTING:
OFFSET

FAUXPAS
LEPORELLO

IRIDIUM, A DESIGN COMPANY
FACE TO FACE CATALOG

Our Vision

We are changing the way you communicate. We bring together video, voice and data over your IP, ATM or SONET network to enable interactive video communications and real-time video transport. Crystal clear video. Pure audio with exceptionally low delay. Flexible solutions to fit the way you work. With the quality of technologies like MPEG-2, and the reliability of a dedicated platform, Miranda Media Networks truly brings you **face to face**.

Changing the Face of Communication

Teach

Video expands the reach of educators and the ability of students to learn. With MPEG-2 technology from Miranda Media Networks, universities, schools, and professional colleges are using their resources more effectively. Video networks tie together statewide school systems, giving students better access to unique classes and greater flexibility in course schedules. Educators have access to best-in-class speakers who are no longer limited by geography or rigid availability. Education is about expanding knowledge, and high quality video can provide the connectivity to make it happen.

Empowering Distance Learning

Live

The difference is quality. Medicine is a world of images, and their accuracy can mean life or death. Reliable, interactive MPEG-2 video enables doctors and specialists to learn, diagnose and treat today's patients more accurately and effectively. And video has become an invaluable part of the critically important teaching process for medical students and interns. In short - video communications can bring the knowledge of experts to those who need it.

Making a Difference in Diagnosis

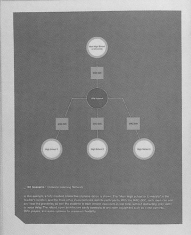

CANADA

ART DIRECTOR:
MARIO L'ÉCUYER

DESIGNER:
JEAN-FRANÇOIS
PLANTE

PHOTOGRAPHER:
HEADLIGHT
INNOVATIVE IMAGERY

CLIENT:
MIRANDA MEDIA
NETWORKS

SOFTWARE AND
HARDWARE:
ILLUSTRATOR
PHOTOSHOP
QUARKXPRESS
MAC 7500

MATERIALS:
EUROART SILK

PRINTING:
BEAUREGARD
PRINTERS

ART DIRECTOR:
EMERY VINCENT
DESIGN

DESIGNER:
EMERY VINCENT
DESIGN

CLIENT:
MACQUARIE FUNDS
MANAGEMENT

AUSTRALIA

EMERY VINCENT DESIGN
INTELLIGENT SOLUTIONS

BAKKEN CREATIVE CO.

Vintners Inn Brochure

ART DIRECTOR:	DESIGNER:	CLIENT:	TOOLS:	MATERIALS:
Michelle Bakken	Gina Mondello	Vintners Inn	Adobe Illustrator	Strathmore Pastelle

Here, having only five senses just doesn't seem fair.

Trade the weight of the world for the weight of a down duvet.

VOICE
Education Brochure

ART DIRECTORS:	DESIGNERS:	CLIENT:	TOOLS:	MATERIALS:
Anthony Deleo	Anthony Deleo	Colour Cosmetica	Macromedia Freehand	Pacesetter Laser
Scott Carslake	Scott Carslake		QuarkXPress	250 gsm (cover)
				Pacesetter Laser
				110 gsm (text)

The historic chapel, overlooking the resort's tropical grounds and beaches, exudes an aura of romance and enchantment that is perfect for weddings and renewal of vows.

Outdoor reception areas and contemporary conference facilities provide a choice of venues for all occasions, with the assurance that One&Only Palmilla's experienced staff will create an atmosphere of impeccable service and hospitality.

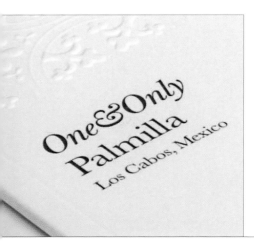

One&Only
Palmilla
Los Cabos, Mexico

PENTAGRAM DESIGN/SF
Sales Brochure

ART DIRECTOR:	DESIGNER:	CLIENT:	TOOLS:
Brian Jacobs	Takayo Muroga	One + Only Resorts	Adobe Photoshop
			Adobe Illustrator
			QuarkXPress

*A luxurious
new awakening*

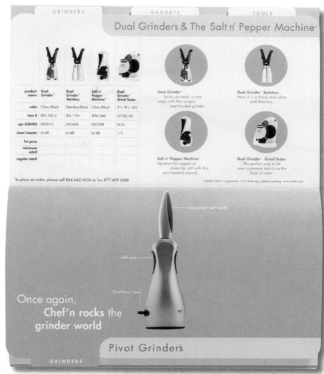

HORNALL ANDERSON DESIGN WORKS, INC.

Chef'n Catalog

ART DIRECTORS:	DESIGNERS:	CLIENT:	TOOLS:	MATERIALS:
Kathy Saito	Sonja Max	Chef'n	Adobe Photoshop	Mohawk Superfine
Jack Anderson	Alan Copeland		QuarkXPress	80 lb (cover)
Lisa Cerveny				

Baby Talk

The Target® Guest will not only pass-on her hazel eyes and curly hair to her new baby, she'll also pass along her sense of style, she'll choose her baby's outfits as carefully as she chooses her own. She'll start encouraging her baby's interests at an early age and make sure her surroundings are safe as well as nurturing. Baby will go wherever mommy does: Shopping, out to lunch and sometimes to work. Don't be surprised to find them both in baby aerobics class.

The Target Lullaby Club® has welcomed more than 4,000,000 bundles of joy.

40% of guests have children under 18 at home.

43% of guests with children have children under 8.

22% are between 18 and 34 years old.

GRAPHICULTURE

Getting to Know . . .

ART DIRECTOR:	CLIENT:	TOOLS:	MATERIALS:
Cheryl Watson	Target	Adobe Illustrator QuarkXPress	dull coated stock

Who is The Core Guest?

Who shops at Target®? The answer is both simple and complex. She's a unique individual (80% are female) who's upscale (median household income of $54,000) and educated (40% have graduated from a 4-year college). When she's not working, you'll find her in her suburban home raising a family (40% have children) and pursuing a variety of interests (41% enjoy gardening). But she's much more than statistics. She's style conscious and aware of trends. She values her time and her opinions. And her life is about to change in a big way. Get to know her and you'll know what she's looking for.

Getting to know the Target® Guest

THE POINT GROUP

Upscale Real Estate Brochure

ART DIRECTOR:
David Howard

DESIGNER:
Cassandra Zimmerman

CLIENT:
W Hotel & Residences

TOOLS:
Adobe Photoshop
Adobe Illustrator
QuarkXPress

MATERIALS:
Domtar Solutions
Carrera white

Getting your message across the world is no easy task. There are many potential pitfalls. It's easy to use the wrong inflection, cause offence, or waste your money. When you're co-ordinating people and projects thousands of miles away, there's plenty of scope for misunderstandings.

Verbatim provides a total solution for companies who want to make their words count in different countries. Though we pride ourselves on the quality of our translation services, our comprehensive language management offer goes much further than just the words. It includes planning, production, logistics and distribution. So we can take a project all the way from the drawing board and right into your target audience's hands.

With Verbatim, you can be sure your words say the right thing at the right time.

> Could your life be made easier?
Few companies have the capability or resources to manage international communications. As well as careful co-ordination, they need local knowledge and dedicated teams in different parts of the world. But Verbatim knows how to smooth the whole process. We're experts in the field, and bring continuity and efficiency to even the most complex projects. Deal with us, and we can deal with everything else for you.

HAT-TRICK DESIGN
Verbatim Brochure

ART DIRECTORS:	DESIGNERS:	CLIENT:	TOOLS:	MATERIALS:
Gareth Howat	Jim Sutherland	Verbatim	Adobe Photoshop	Skye Brilliant White
David Kimpton	Adam Giles		QuarkXPress	
Jim Sutherland				

> Are your words digestible?
Mistranslations can be entertaining ('frozen coolpiece' anybody?). But not when they affect your business. Verbatim makes sure that your messages come across loud, clear and consistently in different territories, in any media. This immediately shows you're serious, switched on and thorough. After all, the quality of your communication is a reflection of the quality of your product.

> Do you mean what you say?
Tone, nuance and emphasis can easily get lost in translation, which is why Verbatim sources its translators so carefully. We use local mother-tongue translators with relevant technical and industry knowledge. And we learn from each project, building glossaries of technical terms and specialist words and phrases that may crop up in the future.

MARIUS FAHRNER DESIGN
Kitchen Brochure for a Designer

ART DIRECTOR:
Marius Fahrner

DESIGNER:
Marius Fahrner

CLIENT:
Ulrike Urages

TOOLS:
Macromedia Freehand

MATERIALS:
Noblesse 300 g naturel
Classen Paper (cover)
Maxi Satin 200 g white
Igepa (text)

USINE DE BOUTONS
TRAVEL BOOK

ART DIRECTOR:
Lionello Borean

DESIGNERS:
Lionello Borean
Chiara Grandesso

CLIENT:
INVICTA SpA

TOOLS:
Adobe Illustrator

NO.PARKING

Presentation Brochure for Franchising Store (single sheets and folder)

ART DIRECTOR:	DESIGNER:	CLIENT:	TOOLS:	MATERIALS:
Caterina Romino	Caterina Romino	Iojo—Body Objects	QuarkXPress	Magnomatt 120 g

ANTFARM INC. (CHANGING TO KAMPER BRANDS)

Stevens Square Condos

DESIGNERS:	CLIENT:	TOOLS:
Dan Behrens	Real Estate Development	Adobe Photoshop
Patrick Crowe	Group	Adobe Illustrator

**ANTFARM INC.
(CHANGING TO KAMPER BRANDS)**

Rossmor True Lofts

DESIGNERS:
Dan Behrens
Patrick Crowe

CLIENT:
PAK Properties

TOOLS:
Adobe Photoshop
Adobe Illustrator

MATERIALS:
four-color process
Pantone 877
spot varnish

butter
cheese
cream
ice cream
milk
new new dairy culture
yogurt

Dairy
The food of life

PERKS DESIGN PARTNERS

Dairy Culture Educational Kit

ART DIRECTOR:	DESIGNER:	CLIENT:	TOOLS:
Chris Perks	Maurice Lai	Dairy Australia	Adobe Illustrator QuarkXPress

GRAPHICULTURE

Swell—Simple Solutions

ART DIRECTOR:
Cheryl Watson

CLIENT:
Target

TOOLS:
Adobe Photoshop
Adobe Illustrator
QuarkXPress

MATERIALS:
coated paper

TRACY DESIGN COMMUNICATIONS
Jennifer-Anne Promotional Brochure

ART DIRECTOR:	DESIGNER:	CLIENT:	TOOLS:
Jan Tracy	Patrick Simon	Jennifer-Anne	Adobe Illustrator
			QuarkXPress

Tasman Bay Olives Ltd incorporates three olive groves – Beulah Olives, Nelson Olive Grove and Bethany Olive Grove, all situated on the Moutere clays in the Tasman Bay region of New Zealand. The Moutere clay is gaining increasing recognition for producing superior flavour for many types of horticultural crops such as wine, apples, and olives. The combination of these ideal growing conditions and high sunshine in the Nelson area results in a premium quality olive oil.

Tasman Bay Olives is primarily focused on the premium Italian varieties. Tests by the Cawthron Institute on Elovi Olive Oil show low acidity levels of between 0.05% to 0.17%.

New Zealand Freshness with an Italian Flavour

ELOVI | OLIVE | OIL

the best of both worlds

Elovi

LLOYDS GRAPHIC DESIGN LTD

Olive Oil Producer Promotional Brochure

ART DIRECTOR:
Alexander Lloyd

DESIGNER:
Alexander Lloyd

CLIENT:
Tasman Bay Olives/Elovi
Olive Oil

TOOLS:
Adobe Photoshop
Macromedia Freehand

MATERIALS:
matte textured stock
220 gsm

LISKA + ASSOCIATES, INC.

The Cass Gilbert Brochure

ART DIRECTOR:	DESIGNERS:	CLIENT:	TOOLS:	MATERIALS:
Tanya Quick	Tanya Quick	Douglas Elliman	Adobe Photoshop	Mohawk Superfine soft
	Fernando Munoz	The Cass Gilbert	Adobe Illustrator	white smooth 100 lb
			QuarkXPress	(cover)

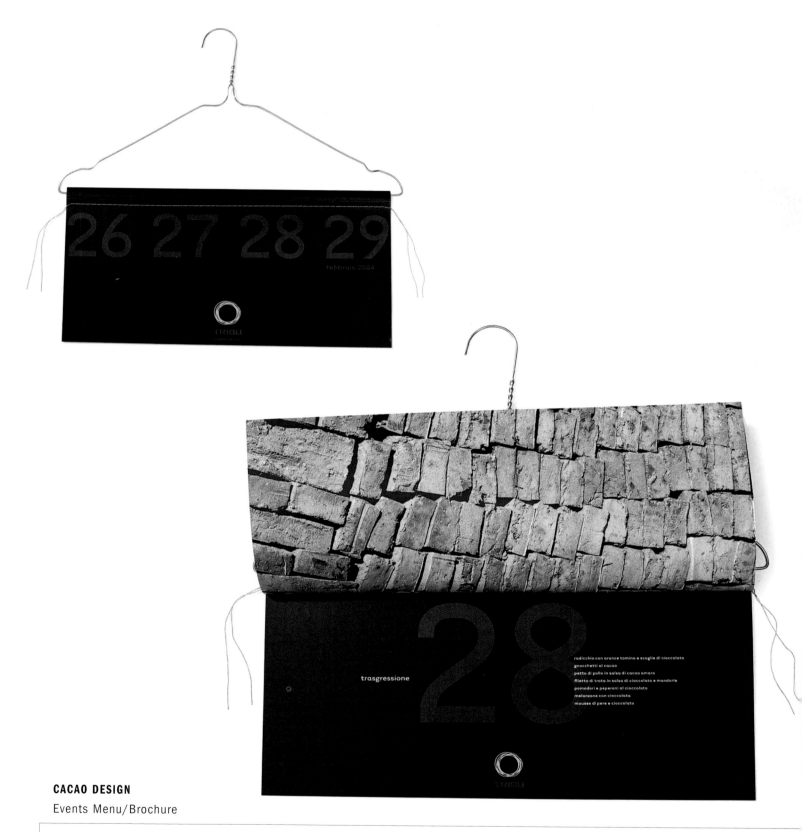

CACAO DESIGN

Events Menu/Brochure

ART DIRECTOR:	DESIGNER:	CLIENT:	TOOLS:
Creative Team	Anna Carbone	Tribu	Adobe InDesign

USINE DE BOUTONS

TEKWAY

ART DIRECTOR:	DESIGNERS:	CLIENT:	TOOLS:
Lionello Borean	Lionello Borean	INVICTA SpA	Adobe Illustrator
	Chiara Grandesso		

Wield your superpowers wisely.

What the program is:
• Front-line employee empowerment
• A change in operating policy and procedures
• A way to add value to our relationship with our Members
• A way to create opportunity for our business and for employees

What it is not:
• A promotional campaign
• A gift to our Members
• A way to please every Member, every time
• An expense account

What you can give:
Use your creativity and resources to identify gestures of varied potency. Here are some examples to guide your team.
• Removal of one Emergency Road Service event
• Membership enrollment, dues, or upgrade waiver
• Removal of a $10 returned check charge

What you cannot give:
• Changes to payment terms
• Changes to Membership by-laws
• Changes to rates upon which insurance premiums are based
• Changes to premium amounts or policy reinstatement

Accountability
Each front-line employee will be empowered to provide gestures up to $100 in value without management approval. Giving gestures is not an exact science. Sometimes it requires sizing up a situation and making a judgment call. Along the way managers and/or supervisors will be there for you, discussing the actions you've taken, offering guidance, and overseeing your monthly performance report. Together you will help to ensure that AAA's new empowerment policy is working the way it is intended to work.

Even superheroes need a little guidance now and then.

Let's see to it that Members always come first.

You've broken free of irksome approvals.
Now go make the world a better place.

About your new superpowers:

Frontline employees, like you, have been telling us lately that you'd like more power. But not just any powers ... special powers. Congratulations! Your super-signal was received and you now have the ability to create the most loyal and satisfied customers in the entire universe.

Wield your new power wisely: ask yourself the following questions before offering a AAA goodwill gesture. Interestingly enough, they're the same questions that managers used to ask themselves before granting approval. The difference is you can do it better, stronger, and faster.

Question One:
Is the solution good for business?

Consider the potential effect on our business of a Member's dissatisfaction. Is this a Member we should make a special effort to keep? Factors like the depth of a Member's relationship with AAA and the number of years he or she has been a Member can signal the importance of a little extra attention.

For example, a 15-year Member who insures both home and auto with us, and who frequently books trip through Travel Services, is a very valuable Member. It would make sense to increase the value of a goodwill gesture for a Member like this. On the other hand, if a Member makes frequent Emergency Road Service calls and insurance claims or if they have a history of payments returned by the bank, he or she may actually be costing us money and making a gesture of any sort may be inappropriate.

In the end, it comes down to how much benefit a Member offers AAA. In other words, do they deserve a superhero's rescue?

CSAA CREATIVE
SERVICES
**Your New Super-
powers Booklet**

Art Director:
Virginia Vovchuk
Designer:
Jeff Carino
Client:
CSAA Sales & Service
Software:
Adobe InDesign
Paper/Materials:
Starwhite Vicksburg
(Fox River)

FLORE VAN RYN
**Catalog / First
Collection Wild-
spirit Furnitures**

Art Director:
Flore Van Ryn
Designer:
Flore Van Ryn
Client:
Wildspirit
Software:
Adobe InDesign
Paper/Materials:
Coated matte 350 gsm
(cover), 150 gsm (text)

HARTFORD
DESIGN, INC.
**Jazz Masters
Promotion**

Art Director:
Tim Hartford
Designers:
Lisa Ermatinger,
Judith Miller
Client:
Nimrod Systems
Software:
QuarkXPress
Paper/Materials:
Potlatch McCoy

SAGMEISTER INC.
Anni Kuan
Brochure, Gold

Art Director:
Stefan Sagmeister
Designer:
Ariane Spanari
Client:
Anni Kuan
Software:
Adobe CS
Paper/Materials:
Newsprint,
gold pieces

FLORE VAN RYN
**Donaldson /
Fashion Catalog**

Art Director:
Flore Van Ryn
Designer:
Flore Van Ryn
Client:
Donaldson
Software:
Adobe InDesign
Paper/Materials:
Munken Lynx 300 gsm
(cover), 150 gsm (text)

We want to be at the heart

Make a paper heart:

innovations. They become evangelists for it. They value it and what it stands for over what it costs. When you love a brand, you follow it into new places.

HP Brand Innovation Lab. Create experiences people love.™

3

+ = everything is possible
hp

In today's competitive business environment, we know our brand is among our most valuable

To build a brand th
we must first build a

We're working to create a company of people whose
customers forges a sense of community, fosters morale and spe
innovation and collaboration.

To that end, we bring people together from across our company to share
ideas and to foster new ways of thinking and working. We lead workshops
where teams collaborate to innovate experiences. We bring in compelling
thought leaders for talks and workshops. We take groups on field trips to
learn from some of the most-loved brands and most compelling brand
experiences in the world. We create a virtual community where people can
participate in our journey. And we share what we hear, read and learn so
that together we can build a brand experience that creates love.

HP Brand Innovation Lab. Create experiences people love.™

13

INSPIRE HEARTS
SPARK COLLABORATION
OPEN MARKETS
UNDERSTAND LIVES
PROVOKE IDEAS
FIND OPPORTUNITIES
SHIFT THINKING
EXPLORE POSSIBILITIES
SHARE KNOWLEDGE
INNOVATE EXPERIENCES
FUEL GROWTH

HP Brand Innovation Lab

HP Brand Innovation Lab. Create experiences people love.™

MIRIELLO
GRAFICO INC.
**Hewlett Packard
Brand Innovation**

Designer:
Dennis Garcia
Client:
Hewlett Packard
Software:
Adobe Illustrator
Paper|Materials:
Carnival 80 lb text

300MILLION
Advocate Paper Works

Art Director:
Nigel Davies
Designer:
Natalie Turner
Client:
Tullis Russell
Software:
QuarkXPress, OSX
Paper|Materials:
Advocate

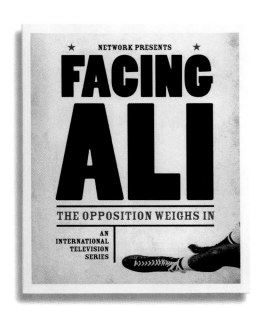

FACING ALI

NETWORK PRESENTS

THE OPPOSITION WEIGHS IN

AN INTERNATIONAL TELEVISION SERIES

SUBPLOT
DESIGN INC.
Facing Ali

Art Directors:
Roy White,
Matthew Clarke
Designer:
Roy White
Client:
Network
Productions Inc.
Paper/Materials:
Pegasus

I CALL IT THE ANCHOR PUNCH
PEOPLE DON'T SEE IT. IT'S SO FAST
MUHAMMAD ALI

SYNOPSIS

WITHOUT QUESTION, THERE HAS BEEN NO GREATER STAR IN THE HISTORY OF THE SPORT THAN

MUHAMMAD ALI

EVEN BEFORE HE WON THE HEAVYWEIGHT CHAMPIONSHIP OF THE WORLD WITH AN UNTHINKABLE UPSET OF SONNY LISTON IN MIAMI BEACH IN 1964, HE HAD SHOWN THAT HE HAD THE MAKINGS OF A VERY DIFFERENT KIND OF ATHLETIC CELEBRITY.

GREAT CHAMPIONS

AND "TOMATO CANS", NOHOPERS AND A FEW MEN WHO BEAT ALI

EACH MAN TELLS A DIFFERENT STORY WHETHER IT BE

TRIUMPHANT ★ TRAGIC
ANGRY
HILARIOUS ★ UPLIFTING

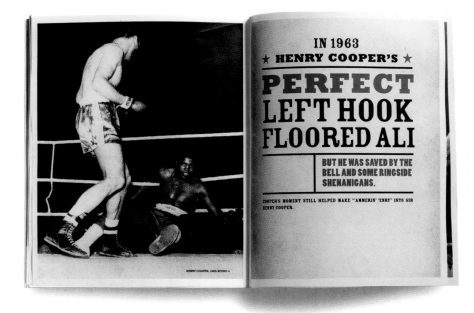

IN 1963
★ HENRY COOPER'S ★

PERFECT LEFT HOOK FLOORED ALI

BUT HE WAS SAVED BY THE BELL AND SOME RINGSIDE SHENANIGANS.

COOPER'S MOMENT STILL HELPED MAKE "'AMMERIN' 'ENRY" INTO SIR HENRY COOPER.

HENRY COOPER, 1963. ROUND 4

MICHAL GRANIT
DESIGN STUDIO
Fashion Catalog

Art Director:
Michal Granit
Illustrator:
Orit Bergman
Client:
Comme il faut
Software:
Freehand,
Adobe Photoshop

the nienkämper store

BLOK DESIGN
Nienkamper
Brochure

Art Director:
Vanessa Eckstein
Designer:
Vanessa Eckstein
Client:
Nienkamper
Paper/Materials:
Beckett Expression
130 lb

SEGURA INC.
Crop (Large Size Brochure)

Art Director:
Carlos Segura
Designers:
Carlos Segura,
Dave Weik,
Chris May,
Tnop
Client:
Corbis
Software:
Adobe InDesign,
Adobe Photoshop,
Adobe Illustrator

ICO DESIGN
CONSULTANCY
**Freehold Property
Brochure**

Art Director:
Andy Spencer
Designer:
Andy Spencer
Client:
Hammerson
Software:
Adobe InDesign
Paper/Materials:
Naturalis

16 – 11
Park Lane's most
prestigious address

**100 Park Lane is rich in
architectural heritage.**

In 1827, John William Ward,
son of William Ward, Viscount
Dudley and Ward, commissioned
the architect William Atkinson
to design and build the first
Dudley home on this site.

The original Dudley House
picture gallery, shown here
in its former glory.

Mayfair's superb location
is popular with the capital's
discerning residents and
visitors alike

100 Park Lane is surrounded
by neighbours of the highest
calibre: from international
corporations to five-star hotels,
and the best in fine dining,
entertainment and luxury retail.

Many original Regency and
Early Victorian interior details
remain, adding to 100 Park
Lane's character.

Some of the building's existing
art work – including some fine
work by Joshua Reynolds –
is also available.

Portraits of
Victorian Dudley
and Lady Ward
hang on the
main staircase

166 THE BEST OF THE BEST OF BROCHURE DESIGN

BLOK DESIGN
Intento 1

Art Director:
Vanessa Eckstein
Designers:
Vanessa Eckstein,
Mariana Contegni
Client:
Blok Design
Software:
Adobe Illustrator CS
Paper/Materials:
Starwhite, Sirus
Smooth, 130 lb (Fox
River)

A LANDMARK CONCEPT WITHOUT EQUAL, A PRIME INVESTMENT OPPORTUNITY WITHOUT RIVAL

On the eastern end of the unspoiled island of Sentosa, located just off the southern coast of the thriving city-state of Singapore, within a stone's throw of the bustling central business district, an extraordinary residential enclave is in the midst of emerging.

Showcasing a unique concept that blends residential, commercial and marina facilities in the form of an integrated waterfront resort, Sentosa Cove introduces a truly magnificent oceanfront lifestyle and community without any equal in the region. Complete with its own fascinating Marina Village, the charming development stands in sharp contrast to the hustle and bustle of cosmopolitan, urban Singapore.

KINETIC
SINGAPORE
**Coral Island
Property Brochure**

Art Directors:
Leng Soh, Pann Lim,
Roy Poh
Designers:
Leng Soh, Pann Lim,
Roy Poh
Client:
Hobee Group
Software:
Freehand,
Adobe Photoshop
Paper/Materials:
Matte art paper, card,
board

Art Director:
Vanessa Eckstein
Designers:
Vanessa Eckstein,
Vanesa Enriquez,
Mariana Contegni
Client:
Jose Cuervo
Software:
Adobe Illustrator
Paper/Materials:
Sundance Smoke and
Ultrawhite Smooth
(Fox River)

TAXI STUDIO LTD
**Serious on the
Outside...**

Art Directors:
Ryan Wills,
Spencer Buck
Designers:
Alex Bane, Karl Wills,
Luke Manning,
Olly Guise
Client:
Science Museum
Software:
QuarkXPress,
Adobe Photoshop,
Adobe Illustrator
Paper/Materials:
Gardapat 13 150 gsm

TAXI STUDIO LTD
Originals
Brochures

Art Director:
Ryan Wills
Designers:
Olly Guise,
Spencer Buck
Client:
Clarks
Software:
QuarkXPress

STILRADAR
**The Grip
Quadrants**

Art Directors:
Raphael Pohland,
Simone Winter
Designers:
Raphael Pohland,
Simone Winter
Client:
Grip AG - Technische
Textilkollktionen
Software:
Freehand
Paper|Materials:
Conqueror 160 gsm,
250 gsm

DIE GRIP QUADRANTEN | Q4. LOGISTIK & SERVICE: DER TRANSPARENZ QUADRANT
THE GRIP QUADRANTS | Q4. LOGISTICS & AFTER SALES: THE TRANSPARENCY QUADRANT

NACH DER LIEFERUNG SCHLUSS ?

Laster, Schiff, Flugzeug: Ihrer Ware stehen alle Wege aus der Fertigung in Ihr Lager oder Logistikzentrum offen. An dieser Stelle gilt besonders, daß Qualität mit Transparenz und Information eng verbunden ist. Unsere Spediteure und Logistikexperten wissen immer, wo Ihre Ware im Moment ist und auf welchem Weg sie sich befindet. Egal, ob auf Container- oder Stückgutfrachter aus Shanghai, Planenzug aus Istanbul oder Leichtfahrzeug bei der Einzelverteilung, für uns endet die Verantwortung für das Produkt noch lange nicht mit dem Abgangsdatum und auch nicht mit dem termingerechten Eintreffen in Ihrem Lager. Mit unserer Verpflichtung für die von uns angebotene Qualität stehen wir bei Beanstandungen mit unserer eigenen Reklamationsabteilung Ihrem Service-Team kompetent zur Seite.

RIGHT IN TIME – RIGHT AT YOUR HAND

Regardless the vehicel – vessel, aircraft or truck: Your goods have every choice to meet your timelines. At this point in the textile value chain quality and informational transparency prove to be a critical part of procurement and planning. Without knowing the whens and the wheres, an effective supply chain management simply is hard to achieve. In close partnership with logistical experts we take the responsibility to deliver in time, at the right place. Even after that we care seriously about quality – our service people are here to team up with your claims department to solve even the most difficult consumers complaints and deescalate the harshest product related issues.

300MILLION
Naturalis
Uncoated
Brochure

Art Directors:
Nigel Davies,
Dom Bailey,
Martin Lawless
Client:
Tullis Russell
Software:
QuarkXPress, OSX
Paper/Materials:
Naturalis

Le Mille
e una Carta
*The Thousand
and One Papers*

Double Face

BURGO

BRUNAZZI
& ASSOCIATI
**Brochures for
Burgo Papers**

Art Director:
Andrea Brunazzi
Designer:
Matteo Marucco
Client:
Cartiere Burgo
Software:
QuarkXPress,
Freehand
Paper/Materials:
Paper and cardboard

A slice of forest,
a toasted beach,
two or three meadows,
a cup of dew.
What is Progress having
for breakfast this morning?

GEORGINAGOODMAN SS05 MADE IN LOVE

ALOOF DESIGN
**Georgina
Goodman Spring/
Summer**

Art Director:
Sam Aloof
Designer:
Andrew Scrase
Client:
Georgina Goodman
Software:
Adobe Illustrator,
Adobe Photoshop
Paper/Materials:
Colorplan
& Zen GF Smith

The people are really nice here.

And other nasty rumors about us.

1 Summer associates are just as valued as partners.

It's hard to know who to kiss up to.

CAHAN & ASSOCIATES
Pillsbury Winthrop Rumors Brochure

Art Director:
Bill Cahan,
Michael Braley
Designer:
Michael Braley
Client:
Pillsbury Winthrop
Shaw Pittman

3 You will work directly with clients early on in your career.

Maybe not week one, but year one. Don't worry, we are behind you.

careers.pillsburylaw.com

2 Summer associates are included in real deals.

It isn't all filet mignon and box seats.

careers.pillsburylaw.com

Art Director:
Nessim Higson
Designer:
Nessim Higson
Client:
Lion Gate Films
Software:
Adobe Photoshop,
Adobe Illustrator

CEM ERUTKU
TASARIM
STUDYOSU - C375
Hotel Brochure

Art Director:
N. Cem Erutku
Designer:
N. Cem Erutku
Client:
Ourco Tourism
Software:
Adobe Photoshop,
Freehand
Paper/Materials:
Sappi 300 gsm

ICO DESIGN
CONSULTANCY
**Freehold Property
Brochure**

Art Director:
Vivek Bhatia
Designer:
Vivek Bhatia
Client:
Bath + Bath
Software:
Adobe InDesign,
Adobe Photoshop
Paper/Materials:
Naturalis, Curious
(main brochure),
Redeem, Curious
(plans book),
Flockage (box)

SEA
Staverton
Brochure

Art Director:
Bryan Edmondson
Designer:
Stuart L Bailey
Client:
Staverton
Software:
QuarkXPress,
Adobe Photoshop
Paper/Materials:
PVC (cover),
Paralux (text)

PAST, PRESENT & FUTURE

DOWLING DESIGN
& ART DIRECTION
**Promotional
Booklet**

Art Director:
John Dowling
Designer:
John Dowling
Client:
Future Designs
Software:
QuarkXPress
Paper/Materials:
Neptune Unique
(Fenner), Colorplan
Ebony (GF Smith)

When we think of history, we think about the debt we owe to the inventor of the light bulb, Thomas Alva Edison.

A true pioneer, Edison gave us many inventions, including the phonograph, the kinescope, centralised power systems (electricity generators) and, of course, the light bulb... or did he?

In 1809, Humphry Davy, an English chemist, invented the first electric light. 26 years later, James Bowman Lindsey used a prototype light bulb to demonstrate his constant electric lighting system.

Henricg Globel, a German watchmaker, invented the first true light bulb in 1854, with a carbonised bamboo filament in a glass bulb. In 1875, Henry Woodward and Matthew Evans patented a light bulb design.

Who knows what the future may bring? You can rest assured that here at FUTURE Designs, we'll be keeping abreast of any further developments, and will continue to innovate in our own field, like Davy, Globel, and Edison before us.

With exceptional engineering and innovative yet appropriate lighting solutions... the future is light.

22

Those who prefer an area less crowded and less expensive than other downtown neighborhoods enjoy living side-by-side with the great amenities and world-class institutions that define the city. Nestled just south of the Sears Tower and steps away from the shores of Lake Michigan, Printers Square offers walking distance proximity to many of the city's leading attractions, public green spaces, the Museum Campus, Culture Coast and great universities. Printers Row boasts architectural treasures, jazz & blues clubs, galleries and bookstores, boutiques and restaurants. This area is also home to the Auditorium Theater and the Spertus Museum of Judaica, facing Grant Park on South Michigan Avenue.

PRINTERS ROW SHOPPING

Printers Row is a haven for book lovers. Sandmeyer's, a Printers Row landmark, is a cozy family-owned and -operated bookstore established in 1982. Visitors to Printers Row Fine & Rare Books will find rare books in rare surroundings, including high quality antiquarian books consisting of classics in world literature, philosophy and the natural sciences. There is even a private viewing room in which patrons may examine books undisturbed. It is a bibliophile's dream. A short walk north you'll find Prairie Avenue Book Shop, the largest architectural bookstore in the world, with a comprehensive inventory of books on architecture, design, technology and related fields.

The South Loop Marketplace, located on Roosevelt Road between Clinton and Canal Streets, opened in 1998. This grocery-anchored retail center features a Dominick's Finer Foods as well as other convenient in-line tenants. The success of this center has turned Roosevelt Road into a developing retail corridor. A Super Target has recently been built, while Home Depot and Whole Foods are actively pursuing land sites in the area. See pages 29 and 30 for a comprehensive listing of shops in the area.

The State Street shopping district is less than four blocks northeast of Printers Row. State Street is home to Chicago's largest retailers including the famous flagship stores of Marshall Field's and Carson Pirie Scott, and the new Sears store. Many national specialty stores are located in the State Street district.

FIREBELLY DESIGN
Real Estate Development Brochure

Art Director:
Dawn Hancock
Designers:
Dawn Hancock,
Aaron Shimer,
Antonio Garcia
Client:
JDL Development Corp.
Software:
Adobe Photoshop,
Adobe Illustrator,
Adobe InDesign
Paper/Materials:
New Leaf
Reincarnation Matte

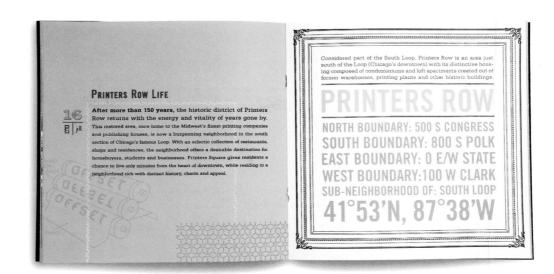

Printers Row Life

16 E/Jul.

After more than 150 years, the historic district of Printers Row returns with the energy and vitality of years gone by. This restored area, once home to the Midwest's finest printing companies and publishing houses, is now a burgeoning neighborhood in the south section of Chicago's famous Loop. With an eclectic collection of restaurants, shops and residences, the neighborhood offers a desirable destination for homebuyers, students and businesses. Printers Square gives residents a chance to live only minutes from the heart of downtown, while residing in a neighborhood rich with distinct history, charm and appeal.

Considered part of the South Loop, Printers Row is an area just south of the Loop (Chicago's downtown) with its distinctive housing composed of condominiums and loft apartments created out of former warehouses, printing plants and other historic buildings.

PRINTERS ROW

NORTH BOUNDARY: 500 S CONGRESS
SOUTH BOUNDARY: 800 S POLK
EAST BOUNDARY: 0 E/W STATE
WEST BOUNDARY: 100 W CLARK
SUB-NEIGHBORHOOD OF: SOUTH LOOP
41°53'N, 87°38'W

TABLE OF CONTENTS

PRINTERS ROW SYNOPSIS

DURING THE DAY, the neighborhood is an easy walk to offices in the Loop, off Michigan Avenue, or the LaSalle Street financial centers. After hours, the district is alive with anything from restaurants, pubs, and blues clubs to coffee shops and bookstores.

It boasts famous blues clubs, eclectic music venues and neighborhood taverns. Its annual book fair, the Chicago Tribune Printers Row Book Fair, gathers authors, poets, speakers and, of course, a great selection of books.

Printers Row is also walking distance to the Spertus Museum of Judaica, the newly reconstructed Soldier Field and Chicago's Museum Campus, with the Field Museum, Adler Planetarium and Shedd Aquarium just blocks away.

Enjoy the excitement of downtown with the serenity of a century old historic district. Printers Square, located at the heart of Printers Row, is just minutes from five-star restaurants, world class shopping on State Street, public green spaces like Grant Park, Dearborn Park, Millennium Park, Harold Washington Library, Chicago's famous Theater District, the "L", Metra, and South Shore Line stations, Sears Tower, US Cellular Field, Burnham Harbor and beautiful Lake Michigan.

PRESS N° 2
A COMPLETE TWO-REVOLUTION PRINTING PRESS UNIT

ATELIER WORKS
**Made in UK
(Promotion for
Product Designers)**

Art Director:
John Powner
Designer:
A. Browne
Client:
Factory Design
Software:
Adobe Photoshop,
QuarkXPress

Portfolio No. 036

Since the beginning of consumerism, the humble tin has been one of the most enduring forms of product design.

A simple, robust method of preserving food, the tin became a brilliant way of advertising and presenting goods and, thanks to Warhol's soup cans, a consumer icon in itself.

We saw a parallel between the tin and our own ambitions; applying simple and robust design solutions to our work, thereby brilliantly influencing consumer culture ourselves.

Light Projects

Appropriate design means appropriate solutions. Even when a product is not intended as the main focus of attention, considered detail, functional benefits and reduced costs all combine to highlight how design can be used as a strategic business tool.

LIEBLING /
WORDS

HAB' GEFUNDEN!

Weich

nuit de noces

LIEBLING /
SPECIMEN   » 07

CHARACTERS
A B C D E F G H I J K L M N O P
Q R S T U V W X Y Z Ä Á Å Â
Ç É È Ê Ö Ó Ò Ô Ü Ú Ù Û Î Ì Ï Ø
a b c d e f g h i j k l m n o p
q r s t u v w x y z ß ä ö ü ø

FIGURES & FORMS
1 2 3 4 5 6 7 8 9 0 € ¢ $ £ ¥
1 2 3 4 5 6 7 8 9 0 & & § #
® © @ % ‰ ™ * + − = ∞

NINA DAVID
KOMMUNIKA-
TIONSDESIGN
Font Report

Art Director:
Nina David
Designer:
Nina David
Client:
Font-o-Rama
Software:
QuarkXPress,
Adobe Photoshop,
Adobe Illustrator
Paper|Materials:
Splendorgel

KAMPER BRANDS
**Brochure for
Factory Conversion
into Lofts**

Art Director:
Patrick Crowe
Designers:
Dan Behrens,
Sarah Anderson
Client:
Trio Development
Software:
Adobe Illustrator,
Adobe Photoshop
Paper/Materials:
130 lb Cougar Double
Thick Cover

KAMPER BRANDS
**Brochure for
Condominium
Project**

Art Director:
Patrick Crowe
Designer:
Sladjana Dirakovi
Client:
The Wall Company
Software:
Adobe Illustrator,
Adobe Photoshop
Paper/Materials:
Domtar Proterra
(Coastal Whites),
cotton bag

RUSSELL
WARREN-FISHER
**Printed Matter
No.1**

Art Director:
Russell Warren-Fisher
Designer:
Russell Warren-Fisher
Client:
Ripe/Park Lane
Software:
QuarkXPress,
Adobe InDesign,
Adobe Photoshop
Paper/Materials:
Consort Royal

SEA
Beyon Brochure

Art Director:
Bryan Edmondson
Designer:
Stuart L Bailey
Client:
Beyon
Software:
QuarkXPress,
Adobe Photoshop
Paper/Materials:
Construction board
(cover), PhoenixMotion Xenon (text)

beyon™ System

The key to the beyon System collection is flexibility. Both the executive and open plan versions can be set up faster than conventional desking systems, more easily and at a fraction of the cost. Not just at your first installation, but everytime you reorganise.

By providing a workspace that is both enlivening and easy to change, beyon helps business embrace new opportunities.

The collection is available in a variety of finishes and sizes and it can be custom made to your requirements.

beyon™ philosophy

To create working environments which are open and inviting, that inspire and motivate, creating feelings of confidence.

Designing clean and contemporary furniture that captures the essence of the modern with the substance and beauty of the classic.

day

leather lane assumes a multitude of identities during the course of each working day. as dawn breaks you can snap into focus with a workout at one of three nearby health clubs or whatever kind of breakfast you want there is a local establishment to suit. sweeps' location is ideal for quickly getting to work in any of london's central business hubs.

as the day wears on, so the gastronomic options increase. smiths buzzes all day long, and the st john bakery offers both freshly baked bread and an exquisite lunch and supper menu. during weekdays, leather lane is home to the thriving 300 year old lunchtime market.

the area also houses facilities to rival, and often surpass, those of any british high street. mcqueens in st john st, while annie khan in hatton garden is well-regarded in the city. nearby hatton garden, london's jewellery capital, features award-winning designer, shaun leane, who crafts bespoke pieces.

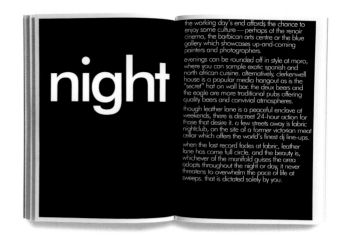

the working day's end affords the chance to enjoy some culture — perhaps at the renoir cinema, the barbican arts centre or the blue gallery which showcases up-and-coming painters and photographers.

evenings can be rounded off in style at moro, where you can sample exotic spanish and north african cuisine. alternatively, clerkenwell house is a popular media hangout as is the "secret" hat on wall bar. the deux beers and the eagle are more traditional pubs offering quality beers and convivial atmospheres.

though leather lane is a peaceful enclave at weekends, there is discreet 24-hour action for those that desire it. a few streets away is fabric nightclub, on the site of a former victorian meat cellar which offers the world's finest dj line-ups.

when the last record fades at fabric, leather lane has come full circle. and the beauty is, whichever of the manifold guises the area adopts throughout the night or day, it never threatens to overwhelm the pace of life at sweeps. that is dictated solely by you.

STUDIO
MYERSCOUGH
**Sweeps Loft
Apartments EC1**

Art Director:
Morag Myerscough
Designer:
Morag Myerscough
Photographer:
Richard Learoyd
Client:
Derwent Valley

Hull
GF Smith
Lockwood Street
Hull HU2 0HL

Telephone
01482 323 503
Facsimile
01482 223 174
Email
info@gfsmith.com

www.gfsmith.com

London
GF Smith
2 Leathermarket
Weston Street
London SE1 3ET

Telephone
020 7407 6174
Facsimile
020 7403 1037
Email
london@gfsmith.com

Paper from GFSmith

Printed on
Monadnock 148gsm

Produced
12/04

Paper from GF Smith

White Book

Paper from GFSmith

SEA
White Book

Art Director:
Bryan Edmondson
Designer:
Ryan Jones
Client:
GF Smith
Software:
QuarkXPress,
Adobe Photoshop
Paper/Materials:
Mixed stock

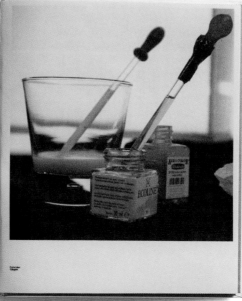

DOWLING DESIGN
& ART DIRECTION
Product Brochure

Art Director:
John Dowling
Designer:
John Dowling
Photographer:
Steve Rees
Client:
Robert Welch
Software:
QuarkXPress
Paper/Materials:
Millenium Silk (Fenner)

HGV
**Wallace Collection
Corporate/Wedding
Brochure**

Art Director:
Pierre Vermeir
Designer:
Tommy Taylor
Client:
Wallace Collection
Software:
Adobe Photoshop,
QuarkXPress
Paper/Materials:
Zanders Medley

RUSSELL
WARREN-FISHER
**Workplace Intel-
ligence Brochure**

Designer:
Russell Warren-Fisher
Client:
Herman Miller
Software:
QuarkXPress,
Adobe Photoshop
Paper/Materials:
Redeem

One Hundred Knightsbridge · London

NB:STUDIO
One Hundred Knightsbridge

Art Directors:
Nick Finney, Ben Stott,
Alan Dye
Client:
Land Securities

HGV
Roast

Art Director:
Pierre Vermeir
Designer:
Pierre Vermeir
Client:
Roast Restaurant
Software:
Adobe Illustrator,
Adobe InDesign
Paper/Materials:
Splendorgel Extra
White (Popset Fawn)

Roast celebrates Britain's
food heritage and our
farming industry. Classical
and modern dishes are
prepared with care and
precision, using the finest
of ingredients – some of
which are sourced by the
stallholders in the market.

A centrepiece attraction
of the restaurant is a large
spit oven that may be
roasting a suckling pig one
day, ribs of beef the next
and wild birds on the third.

Seafood and salads with
wild and organic leaves will
feature strongly on our daily
changing menu alongside
pies and puddings.

We aim to deliver all of this
with charming and efficient
service. We look forward to
welcoming you.

roast

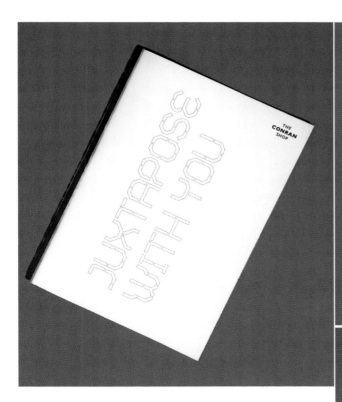

STUDIO
MYERSCOUGH
**Conran Shop
Furniture**

Art Director:
Morag Myerscough
Designer:
Morag Myerscough
Photographer:
Richard Learoyd
Client:
Conran Shop,
Polly Dickens
& Terence Conran

PENTAGRAM
DESIGN, LONDON
**Edmund De Waal
Catalogue**

Art Director:
Angus Hyland
Client:
Blackwell: De Waal

Edmund de Waal A line around a shadow

STUDIO
MYERSCOUGH
Tea Building

Art Director:
Morag Myerscough
Designers:
Morag Myerscough,
Chris Merrick
Photographer:
Richard Learoyd
Client:
Derwent Valley

The end is nigh. Burn all the books. Words are done for. Pictures are the future. If you believe everything you read, you wouldn't be reading. Books would be doorstops and brochures would be shelved. And as for direct mail and magazines, the less said about them the better. But the truth is different.

ink! is a team of copywriters, journalists and communication strategists who believe words can still have a huge impact. We work with design agencies and businesses offering strategic advice for their literature, writing words that jump off the page and making every letter count. Starting here.

MYTTON WILLIAMS
Ink! Promotional Brochure

Art Director:
Bob Mytton
Designer:
Tracey Bowes
Client:
Ink! Copywriters
Software:
Adobe InDesign
Paper/Materials:
Challenger Offset
120 gsm

Words are a little like icebergs. Beneath the elegant bits on the surface is an unseen force holding everything together. In writing, this is the thought behind the words; the strategy that makes your communication stand out. So before we put pen to paper, we pause for a while.

And take a moment to fully understand your aims and challenges, your company's brand values and tone of voice, your audience's attitudes and behaviour. At these opening stages, our strategic thought can really add value. Then, when everything's in place, we start to write.

MIKE
LACKERSTEEN
DESIGN
Beat

Art Director:
Mike Lackersteen
Designer:
Mike Lackersteen
Client:
Heart
Paper/Materials:
Matrisse Avorio
(cover), Neptune
Unique Fenner Paper
(text)

...of sheer luxury and taste

PENTAGRAM
DESIGN, LONDON
**One & Only
Brochure**

Art Director:
John Rushworth
Client:
One & Only

...of excitement and discovery

NONPROFIT,
EDUCATIONAL,
INSTITUTIONAL,
AND HEALTHCARE
BROCHURES

the way **we lived**

New York in Isabella's early years was already the
nation's cultural and financial capital. Yet in 1875,
aseptic surgery was just being introduced, and the
first major school of nursing was only two years old.
In Upper Manhattan, Broadway was a muddy road.
But by 1906, a subway served 191st Street, and by
the 1920s, farmland gave way to apartment houses.
Despite the invention of exercise classes and chain
drugstores, the horse and buggy still delivered the milk.

Lower Broadway, late 1800s

Herald Square, 1906

Nurse tending oxygen tent ›

The milk wagon,
1936

Young women exercising, 1920s

Whelan's Drugstore, 44th Street
and Eighth Avenue, 1936.

Dyckman Farm House, Broadway
and 204th Street, 1890s

DESIGN FIRM › O & J Design Inc.
ART DIRECTORS › Barbara Olejniczak, Lia Camera Mariscal
DESIGNERS › Barbara Olejniczak, Lia Camera Mariscal
ILLUSTRATOR/PHOTOGRAPHER › David Radler
COPYWRITERS › Kalen Blinn, Mimi Koren
CLIENT › Isabella Geriatric Center
TOOLS (SOFTWARE/PLATFORM) › QuarkXpress
PAPER STOCK/PRINTING PROCESS › Cover: three-color; interior: two-

DESIGN FIRM › Zappata Diseñadores S.C.
ART DIRECTOR › Ibo Angulo
DESIGNER › Ibo Angulo
CLIENT › Nuevo Mundo University
TOOLS (SOFTWARE/PLATFORM) › Photoshop, Freehand, Macintosh
PRINTING PROCESS › Offset, couche

EVERYONE
NEEDS A
HERO

The Doctors' Company

DESIGN FIRM > Oh Boy, A Design Company
ART DIRECTOR > David Salanitro
DESIGNER > Ryan Mahar
PHOTOGRAPHER > Scott Goldsmith
COPYWRITERS > Susan Wilkinson, Dana Cooper
CLIENT > The Doctors' Company
PAPER STOCK > Superfine, ultra white smooth

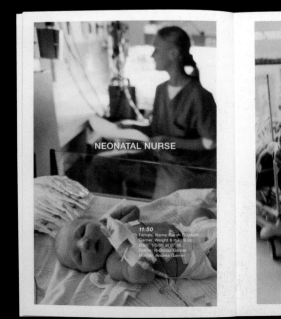

NEONATAL NURSE

11:50
Female. Name: Sarah Elizabeth
Garner. Weight 6 lbs. 8 oz.
Born: 1/5/00 at 07:16.
Father: Nicholas Garner.
Mother: Andrea Garner.

DESIGN FIRM > Shamlian Advertising
ART DIRECTOR > Brian DiRienzi
DESIGNER > Brian DiRienzi
CLIENT > ESF Summer Camps
TOOLS (SOFTWARE/PLATFORM) > Photoshop, Macintosh
PAPER STOCK/PRINTING PROCESS > 4/4

DESIGN FIRM > Gee + Chung Design
ART DIRECTOR > Earl Gee
DESIGNERS > Earl Gee, Fani Chung
PHOTOGRAPHER > Steve Jost
COPYWRITERS > Stephanie Lasenza, Gary Hawk
CLIENT > Alliance Healthcare Foundation
TOOLS (SOFTWARE/PLATFORM) > QuarkXPress, Adobe Illustrator, Photoshop
PAPER STOCK > Potlatch Karma natural 100 lb. text, French Paper Co., Speckletone Madero beach white 70 lb. text
PRINTING PROCESS > Offset lithography, blind embossing

www.thap.net

path!

DESIGN FIRM › Oh Boy, A Design Company
ART DIRECTOR › David Salanitro
DESIGNER › Alice Chang
PHOTOGRAPHER › Tony Stone Images
COPYWRITER › Son Rant
CLIENT › Thap!
PAPER STOCK › Caress eggshell 80 lb.
PRINTING PROCESS › Offset, sheet fed

!augh

Laugh and the whole world laughs with you. Laughing relaxes muscles, increases heart rate, improves the oxygenation of blood and releases positive mood-enhancing endorphins which all lead to longer, healthier and happier lives.

partners in health, healing & hope

The University of Iowa Hospitals and Clinics The University of Iowa College of Medicine

DESIGN FIRM › University of Iowa Foundation
ART DIRECTOR › Theresa Black
DESIGNER › Theresa Black
ILLUSTRATORS/PHOTOGRAPHERS › Jon Van Allen, Diane Hill, Reggie Morrow
COPYWRITER › Claudia Reinhardt
CLIENT › VI Foundation
TOOLS (SOFTWARE/PLATFORM) › Pagemaker, Photoshop, Macintosh
PAPER STOCK › Gilbert Voice
PRINTING PROCESS › Three PMS colors

share
learn
explore
care
hope
understand
believe

WITS

DESIGN FIRM › SamataMason
ART DIRECTOR › Greg Samata
DESIGNER › Kevin Kureger
PHOTOGRAPHERS › Sandro, Martha Brock
CLIENT › WITS (Working in the Schools)
TOOLS (SOFTWARE/PLATFORM) › QuarkXPress, Macintosh
PAPER STOCK › French Speckletone Chipboard,
Appleton Utopia two matt and Springhill Incentive
PRINTING PROCESS › Offset printing, sheet fed

The mission of
Working In The
Schools (WITS)
is to promote ...

DESIGN FIRM > Danette Angerer
ART DIRECTOR > Danette Angerer
DESIGNER > Danette Angerer
ILLUSTRATORS/PHOTOGRAPHERS > Mike Schlotterback, Mark Trade, Rod Bradley, Michael Ask, Jeff Schmatt
COPYWRITER > Elinor Day
CLIENT > Brucemore
TOOLS (SOFTWARE/PLATFORM) > Pagemaker, Macintosh
PAPER STOCK > Dust cover: Environment Desert Storm. Cover: Environment Sedona Red.
Flysheet: U.V./Ultra II sepia interior. Interior stock: Sterling satin.
PRINTING PROCESS > Four-color process, PMS 876 metallic and spot dull varnish
PRINTER > Garner Printing, Des Moines, IA

This was never used for wrapping Sarah's presents.

There are thousands like Sarah. Twenty six per cent of recorded rape victims are children under 16.

What is the FULL STOP Campaign?
The NSPCC launched the FULL STOP Campaign in March 1999. The Campaign has a single aim – to end cruelty to children.

04/00 NSPCC

Dad's belt fitted Adam perfectly.

Without your help cruelty to children will continue. Please join us to stop it.
FULL STOP

RADLEY YELDAR
NSPCC BROCHURE

ART DIRECTOR:	DESIGNER:	PHOTOGRAPHER:	CLIENT:	SOFTWARE AND HARDWARE:	MATERIALS:	PRINTING:
ANDREW GORMAN	KEITH CULLEN	JOHN EDWARDS	NSPCC	QUARKXPRESS MAC	DISTINCTION	FERNEDGE

To stop all cruelty to children FULL STOP.

To stop all cruelty to children FULL STOP.

To stop all cruelty to children FULL STOP.

NSPCC
Cruelty to children must stop FULL STOP

Tim used to see this bat on a regular basis. He's never played baseball in his life.

There are thousands like Tim. Today there are 10,000 children on child protection registers because of serious concerns about physical abuse.

This was never used to secure Joe's nappy.

There are thousands like Joe. The people most likely to die a violent death in the UK are babies under one year old.

Who are NSPCC?

Although the appropriate development of open space and building sites varies by planning precinct, Yale's linear and dispersed campus can be better integrated by judicious attention to campus-wide systems—uses, built form, landscape and open space, circulation, parking, lighting, signage and neighborhood interface.

the Route 34/Oak Street Connector to Chapel Street. A joint effort by the City and Yale could significantly enhance the area by improving the streetscape and expanding arts-related uses, medical uses (both office and clinical), restaurants, retail stores, shops and studios that support the performing and visual arts. Development and improvements should focus on the York and College Street corridors. Yale already has an important presence in this area. It owns several parcels on York Street between Chapel and High Streets. University Towers houses many Yale-related tenants and the Medical Center leases space north of the Route 34/Oak Street Connector. The retail space between George Street and the Air Rights Garage has a high turnover rate that might decrease if quality stores moved in. The University should propose to the City that it convert York and College Streets to two-way traffic, and that it undertake landscaping and lighting programs to improve vehicular access and the pedestrian experience for everyone in the area. Physical improvements and building development along these corridors would reinforce connections between the Central Campus and Medical Center.

These two opportunities, especially when undertaken through joint planning projects by the City of New Haven and the University, would enhance the City and move each significantly closer to the common goal of more fully blending Yale's environment with that of its neighbors.

CAMPUS FRAMEWORK SYSTEMS

Uses
Built Form
Landscape and Open Space
Circulation
Pedestrian
Vehicular
Bicycles
Parking
Signage
Lighting
Neighborhood Interface

POULIN + MORRIS
YALE UNIVERSITY: A FRAMEWORK
FOR CAMPUS

ART DIRECTOR:
RICHARD POULIN

DESIGNER:
AMY KWON

CLIENT:
COOPER,
ROBERTSON &
PARTNERS

SOFTWARE:
QUARKXPRESS

MATERIALS:
MOHAWK
SUPERFINE

PRINTING:
UNIVERSAL
PRINTING

CLARK CREATIVE GROUP
THE STANFORD CARDINAL 90–00

USA

ART DIRECTOR:
ANNEMARIE CLARK

DESIGNER:
NOREEN REI
FUKUMORI

CLIENT:
STANFORD
ATHLETIC DEPT

SOFTWARE:
ILLUSTRATOR
PHOTOSHOP
QUARKXPRESS

MATERIALS:
CENTURA

PRINTING:
HEMLOCK PRINTERS

The Odyssey: History, Transmission, and Performance

Contemporary Women Writers and Stories of Emotion

Doing More than Watching: Big Brother Today

John Singer Sargent and the Triumph and Collapse of Portraiture

Love as Theatre: The Drama of Shakespeare's Sonnets

Information, Anxiety, and the K-12 Classroom

That's My Song! Popular Music and American Culture

Beowulf: Medieval Heroes and Monsters in the Modern World

What is China?

The Information Democracy

2000-01
SEMINARS IN THE HUMANITIES FOR K-12 TEACHERS

teachers *as*
SCHOLARS

Sponsored by Seattle Arts & Lectures and the Simpson Center for the Humanities

DESIGNER:	CLIENT:	SOFTWARE:	MATERIALS:	PRINTING:
KAREN CHENG	SEATTLE ARTS AND LECTURES	ILLUSTRATOR PHOTOSHOP QUARKXPRESS	FINCH FINE COVER + TEXT	2 PMS COLORS

USA

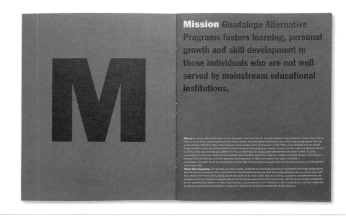

Mission Guadalupe Alternative Programs fosters learning, personal growth and skill development in those individuals who are not well served by mainstream educational institutions.

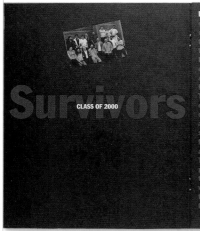

Imagine attending high school while you are pregnant or getting yourself and your child ready for school every morning. Imagine arriving in this country as a teenager and having to learn a second language while taking academic courses required for graduation. Imagine getting a year or more behind your classmates in school, but persevering and graduating anyway. Imagine the pressure and honor of being the first person in your family to graduate.

The 23 students who made up the GAP graduating class of 2000 have lived through situations that some of us can only imagine. They are a group of survivors and left high school just a few weeks ago as seasoned, confident young adults ready to seize their futures. To a person, they know how to set and achieve goals, use their resources, help one another. They are ready. In their words, GAP has been a small place where they got individual attention, where teachers were cool, and where students got along well together. It is a nice thing to think about now that they are gone and we look forward to the beginning of another school year.

Survivors
CLASS OF 2000

ART DIRECTOR:
WILLIAM HOMAN

DESIGNER:
WILLIAM HOMAN

CLIENT:
GUADALUPE
ALTERNATIVE
PROGRAM

MATERIALS:
CLASSIC CREST

PRINTING:
CUSTOM COLOR
PRINTING

WILLIAM HOMAN DESIGN
GUADALUPE ALTERNATIVE PROGRAM

Milestones of the millennium As we move forward into the next century, our goal is to be prepared to meet the needs of all current and future GAP students. We have grown from a one-room house to a building with programs that provide multiple educational opportunities for youth and adults. **We** have reached many milestones this year. On an academic level, our students' scores improved substantially over last year. Culturally, through collaborations and partnerships, students have learned about the richness and diversity of others, the importance of tradition and the need to respect each other. They continue to prepare for the technological advances of the future and the need for communication and computer skills. **We** can achieve these goals because of the commitment and dedication of the staff. Congratulations to Sister Anna Louise Wilson, who will be celebrating her fiftieth anniversary as a School Sister of Notre Dame. She has worked at GAP for 25 years. Her contributions to GAP have been legendary. She has received numerous awards, but what is more important to her is the contact she makes with students in her art classes. **The** board has diligently worked this year to provide the resources for staff members to create an environment that allows each student to reach his or her potential. A new strategic plan has been adopted to position us for the future. We remain committed to the mission of GAP. Karen Thompson, Chair, GAP Board of Directors

Sister Ann

This annual report reviews the year 1999 and, we hope, shows that this agency is secure financially and solid as an educational institution—as it always has been. It also celebrates the graduating class of 2000 and the teachers and support staff who had so much to do with the success of our new-century graduates. We appreciate them and their talents and we also, and in the same breath, appreciate you and your support of GAP. In a unique way, your dedication to our mission is felt here every day, helping us create a place where learning and opportunity are realities.

Thanks

ART DIRECTORS:	DESIGNERS:	CLIENT:	MATERIALS:	PRINTING:
CHIARA GRANDESSO	CHIARA GRANDESSO	CHIARA GRANDESSO	ENVELOPE WITH	CMYK + GOLD INK
LIONELLO BOREAN	LIONELLO BOREAN	LIONELLO BOREAN	EMBOSSED PRINT	+ 1 PANTONE

USINE DE BOUTONS
MAYAPLUM BIRTH
ANNOUCEMENT

ITALY

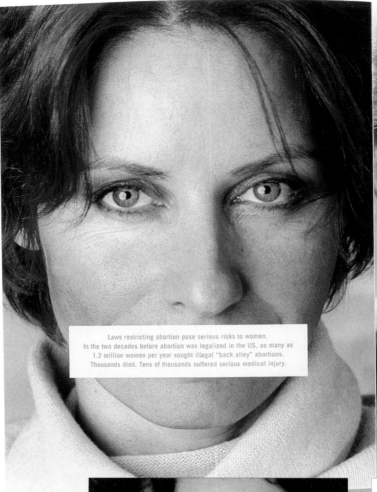

Laws restricting abortion pose serious risks to women.
In the two decades before abortion was legalized in the US, as many as
1.2 million women per year sought illegal "back alley" abortions.
Thousands died. Tens of thousands suffered serious medical injury.

Medically safe, legal abortion has had a profound effect
on the health and well being of American women. Today, abortion
is nearly twice as safe as a penicillin injection.

IT'S ABOUT TIME

BenchMark
NCJW's Campaign to Save Roe

NCJW'S VOICE:
THE VOICE OF THE JEWISH COMMUNITY

FOR OVER A CENTURY THE NATIONAL COUNCIL
OF JEWISH WOMEN HAS BEEN AT THE FOREFRONT
OF SOCIAL CHANGE—COURAGEOUSLY TAKING A
PROGRESSIVE STANCE ON ISSUES SUCH AS
REPRODUCTIVE FREEDOM. TODAY, NCJW IS
THE LEADING JEWISH ORGANIZATION FIGHTING
TO PROTECT THAT FREEDOM.

As Jews, we under-
stand what it means
to have fundamental
rights and liberties
stripped away.

WE CANNOT
BE SILENT ON
THIS ISSUE

92% OF THE JEWISH COMMUNITY
IS PRO-CHOICE

IT IS TIME TO BRING THE POWER AND THE
VOICE OF THAT COMMUNITY TOGETHER

Reproductive rights are closely tied to religious freedom. Women have the right to be respected
as moral decision-makers, able to make choices based on their own beliefs and traditions.
For the courts to impose one religion's view on all of us defies the very meaning of religious liberty.

NCJW'S BENCHMARK C
ALREADY TAKING ACTIO

EDUCATING AND MOBILIZING THOUSAN

LEADING PRO-CHOICE RALLIES AND CO
ACROSS THE COUNTRY

BUILDING STATE COALITIONS

FLYING KEY LEADERS AND SPEAKERS
TO MEET WITH SENATORS

EMPOWERING ONLINE ACTIVISTS VIA A
AN INTERACTIVE WEB SITE

NOW, IT'S YO

LOG ON TO WWW.BENCHM
AND JOIN BENCHMARK TODAY

ART DIRECTOR:	DESIGNER:	CLIENT:	TOOLS:	MATERIALS:
David Schimmel	Susan Brzozowski	National Council of Jewish Women	Adobe Photoshop QuarkXPress	Productolith

THE EROSION OF FREEDOM IS A SLIPPERY SLOPE. IF WE LOSE REPRODUCTIVE RIGHTS, OTHER CORE RIGHTS—LIKE RELIGIOUS LIBERTY AND CIVIL RIGHTS—MAY BE CLOSE BEHIND.

THE FUTURE WILL BE SET BY JUDGES WHO HOLD LIFETIME SEATS ON THE FEDERAL BENCH. ANTI-CHOICE JUDGES ARE ALREADY ATTACKING THE RIGHT TO ABORTION. AND MORE ANTI-CHOICE NOMINEES ARE WAITING IN THE WINGS—POSITIONED TO RENDER DECISIONS THAT WILL DEFINE FREEDOM FOR GENERATIONS TO COME.

The President openly admires staunch anti-choice jurists and is nominating extremists to the federal bench. Senators have a constitutional duty to independently evaluate such nominees. Yet, they have been pressured to rush their decision-making and have, on occasion, been bypassed entirely.

FIND YOUR VOICE. IT'S TIME TO SPEAK OUT AND FIGHT BACK. ON JANUARY 22, 1973 THE SUPREME COURT AFFIRMED WOMEN'S CONSTITUTIONAL RIGHT TO ABORTION IN ITS LANDMARK *ROE V. WADE* RULING. TODAY THIS RIGHT IS UNDER ATTACK IN COURTROOMS ACROSS THE COUNTRY. YOU CAN DO SOMETHING ABOUT IT. TAKE ACTION TODAY, BEFORE IT'S TOO LATE.

IGN IS

EOPLE

Y EVENTS

INGTON, DC

JPDATES, AND

TURN

MPAIGN.ORG

MIRKO ILIĆ CORP.

Massachusetts Lesbian & Gay Bar
Association Brochures

ART DIRECTOR:	CLIENT:	TOOLS:
Mirko Ilić	Massachusetts Lesbian & Gay Bar Association	QuarkXPress

GEORGE TSCHERNY, INC.
Hurra! We Made It—Brochure

ART DIRECTOR:	DESIGNERS:	PHOTOGRAPHER:	CLIENT:	TOOLS:	MATERIALS:
Siles H. Rhodess	George Tscherny	Joseph Sinnot	School of Visual Arts	Adobe Photoshop	Centura white dull
	Matthew Cocco			QuarkXPress	white 80 lb (cover)

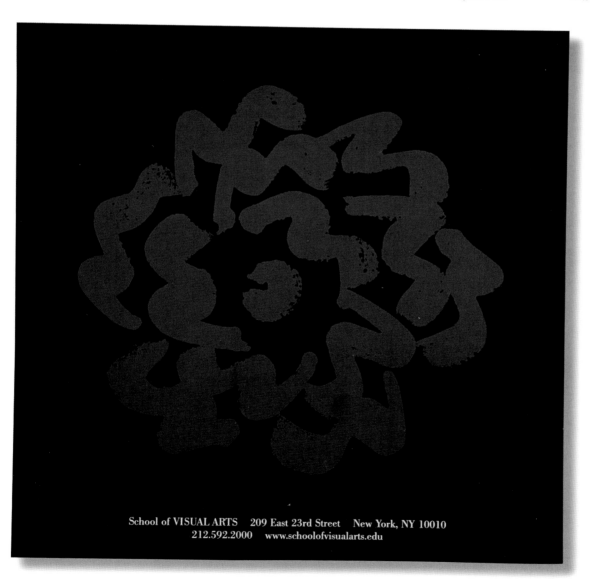

School of VISUAL ARTS   209 East 23rd Street   New York, NY 10010
212.592.2000   www.schoolofvisualarts.edu

HAT-TRICK DESIGN

The Graduate Pioneer Programme

ART DIRECTORS:	DESIGNERS:	CLIENT:	TOOLS:	MATERIALS:
Gareth Howat	David Kimpton	Nesta	Adobe Photoshop	Naturalis
David Kimpton	Jamie Ellul		QuarkXPress	
Jim Sutherland	Mark Wheatcroft			

RUTGERS UNIVERSITY

Rutgers Study Abroad—Recruitment Brochure

ART DIRECTOR:	DESIGNER:	CLIENT:	TOOLS:	MATERIALS:	MATERIALS:
John Van Cleaf	John Van Cleaf	Rutgers Study Abroad	Adobe Photoshop QuarkXPress	French Paper Durotone Butcher, off white 100 lb (cover)	Finch Vanilla Fine 105 lb (text)

ALTERPOP

California Academy of Sciences Brochure

ART DIRECTOR:	DESIGNER:	CLIENT:	TOOLS:
Dorothy Remington	Christopher Simmons	California Academy of Sciences	Adobe Photoshop Adobe InDesign

NESNADNY + SCHWARTZ
Case Western Reserve University
Peter B. Lewis Grand Opening
Dedication Brochure

ART DIRECTORS:	DESIGNERS:	CLIENT:	TOOLS:	MATERIALS:
Mark Schwartz	Michelle Moehler	Case Western Reserve	Adobe Photoshop	Mohawk Option
Michelle Moehler	Gregory Oznowich	University and	Adobe Illustrator	Kromekoteplus
Gregory Oznowich	Stacie Ross	Weatherhead School	QuarkXPress	Benefit
Stacie Ross		of Management		

CARTLIDGE LEVENE
The Business of Design, Design Industry Research

Art Director:
Ian Cartlidge
Designer:
Cartlidge Levene
Client:
Design Council
Software:
Adobe InDesign
Paper/Materials:
Howard Smith (cover),
Think White (text),
McNaughton
Cyclus (text)

HAT-TRICK DESIGN
**The Salvation Army
International Head-
quarters Brochure**

Art Director:
David Kimpton
Designer:
Ben Christie
Client:
The Salvation Army
Software:
QuarkXPress
Paper/Materials:
Bible Paper

The Co-Chairs and Committee of The Magic Ball always do their best to keep the costs to stage the event as low as possible. Through so doing the maximum funds raised can go towards maintaining and developing the charity's crucial work. Central to achieving this is the generosity and support we receive from so many individuals and companies - from the printing of this programme by Fulmar Colour Printing to the design work by Inaria - from the donation of the resources, auction and raffle items to the time and enthusiasm of our team of volunteers, magicians and performers. Each one vital to achieving our objectives.

THANK YOU TO ALL OF OUR SUPPORTERS

DOMESTIC LABOUR ENFORCED IN PERU

Anti-Slavery is committed to eliminating all forms of slavery in today's world. Slavery, servitude and forced labour are violations of individual freedom, which deny basic dignity and fundamental human rights. Anti-Slavery supports today's fight for tomorrow's freedom by exposing current cases of slavery and campaigning for their eradication, supporting the initiatives of local organisations to release people, supporting the prevention and rehabilitation of child domestic workers, and pressing for more effective implementation of international laws against slavery.

David Simpson
Honorary Life Member,
Anti-Slavery International

ANTI-SLAVERY INTERNATIONAL'S MISSION

INARIA
**Colors of the
World**

Art Directors:
Andrew Thomas,
Debora Berardi
Designers:
Andrew Thomas,
Debora Berardi
Client:
Anti-Slavery
International
Paper/Materials:
Hanno Art Silk
200 gsm (text),
Hanno Art Gloss
320 gsm (cover)

POULIN + MORRIS
INC.
**Brooklyn Botanic
Garden, Master Plan**

Designers:
L. Richard Poulin,
Anna Crider
Client:
Brooklyn Botanic
Garden
Software:
Adobe InDesign
Paper/Materials:
Sappi, Lustro Dull

STOLTZE DESIGN
**Harvard Business
School Admissions
Brochure**

Art Director:
Clifford Stoltze
Designer:
Roy Burns
Client:
Harvard Business
School
Software:
QuarkXPress
Paper/Materials:
Finch Fine

you can hear it
in the **voices** of
the students…

Harvard
Business School
is a community
of people engaged
in many
activities focused
on one purpose—
developing
leaders.

HBS PROVIDES US THE OPPORTUNITY TO SIT IN A CLASSROOM WITH
PEOPLE FROM SO MANY COUNTRIES WHO INFORM OUR UNDERSTANDING
OF THE ISSUES THAT FACE THEIR HOMES. I'VE REALIZED HOW
SMALL A SLICE OF GLOBAL LIFE I'D EXPERIENCED AND HOW MANY
THINGS EXIST ABOUT WHICH I'D LIKE TO KNOW MORE.

William D. Rahm

KOLEGRAM
**Canadian Archive
Association
Promotion**

Designer:
Gontran Blais
Client:
Library & Archives
Canada
Paper/Materials:
Domtar Titanium and
Proterra

Art Director:
Richard
Bonner-Morgan
Designer:
Richard
Bonner-Morgan
Photographer:
Richard Learoyd
Client:
London Artscom
Limited
Software:
QuarkXPress
Paper/Materials:
Nimrod Silk

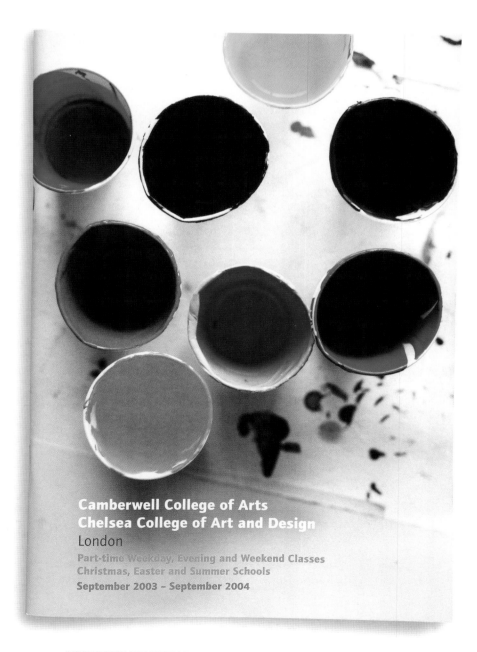

**Camberwell College of Arts
Chelsea College of Art and Design**
London
**Part-time Weekday, Evening and Weekend Classes
Christmas, Easter and Summer Schools
September 2003 – September 2004**

NURSERY: THE CENTER FOR SUSTAINABLE GARDENING

The nursery is the cradle of San Francisco Botanical Garden. There, rare, imported species receive the tender protection they need to survive, and familiar plants are nurtured before taking their place in the Garden. But the garden we love has outgrown the temporary nursery it has relied on since 1960. Our campaign calls for major funding to replace this cold, overcrowded, and deteriorating facility with a modern one — "green" in spirit, function, and design — that merges propagation capabilities with education. This Center for Sustainable Gardening will support our increasingly popular plant sales, which generate revenue for the Society and its programs and send many rare plant specimens home with local gardeners. Relocated for greater safety, efficiency, and accessibility, the Center will enable us to protect and build the one-of-a-kind plant collection that makes our garden great.

JOHN SCHARFFENBERGER,
VICTORIES AND CHOCOLATIER,
CO-CHAIR, CAMPAIGN
LEADERSHIP COMMITTEE

When John Scharffenberger was choosing a wedding garden for his property in Mendocino, he turned to San Francisco Botanical Garden. There, in the secret living library that invited the kitchen garden he created from scratch, John found incredible varieties of the conifers that grow in Northern California and camphellia shrubs that would thrive alongside them.

PENTAGRAM DESIGN,
SAN FRANCISCO

**San Francisco
Botanical Garden**

Art Director:
Kit Hinrichs
Designers:
Belle How,
Jessica Siegel
Client:
The San Francisco
Botanical Garden
Association
Software:
Adobe InDesign

Think about what makes a city great: Is it the spirit and outlook of its people? Its geography? Its history? San Francisco, a great city by any measure, has it all — including one inspiring resource no great city should be without: a botanical garden where people can experience nature, learn about plants and the environment, relax, and seek respite from urban life. Since 1940, San Francisco Botanical Garden at Strybing Arboretum has embodied all that makes San Francisco great — a jewel-like setting, a mild climate in which diversity thrives, a conservation spirit, and a sensibility that cherishes beauty and seeks to share it with others. For the people of the Bay Area, this unique garden is more than a place in Golden Gate Park. It's a place in our hearts, a familiar backdrop for the times of our lives. On its daisy-dotted meadows, we've picnicked or sat sketching a magnificent magnolia in bloom. On its meandering paths, we've contemplated life's big issues, answered a child's questions about nature, or sought inspiration for a home garden, even if it's a window box. However we experience it, this garden reminds us that connecting with and protecting nature — whether we're dedicated gardeners or just admirers of Earth's diverse beauty — makes us more alive. For 50 years, the Botanical Garden Society has augmented public funding to make San Francisco Botanical Garden great. Now, with your help, we can turn San Francisco's garden — the garden we love — into one of the world's finest botanical gardens. This opportunity is unique and perishable, and the time to seize it is now, while we have a vision of what our great city's garden can become and the talented team to bring that vision to life.

SÄGENVIER DESIGN
KOMMUNIKATION
**Attention
Schulden Falle**

Art Director:
Sigi Ramoser
Designers:
Klaus Österle,
Oli Ruhm,
Silvia Keckeis
Client:
AK Vorarlberg

'I was attracted by the one-year programme and the opportunity to experience French and Asian culture. In a world that continues to get closer, INSEAD stands out as an example of how students and faculty drawn from across the globe can come together to make an unforgettable experience. When I came to INSEAD a year ago, I never expected to leave with the diversity and depth of friendships I have today'. **Monisha Dillon, 25 (United Kingdom)**

'I chose INSEAD because of the diversity of the student body. I had good friends who were alums who spoke highly of the place. Also, I had met their friends and felt they were broadminded and internationally orientated. The ability to move geographies and, at my relatively mature age, the one year programme, also appealed to me. It was a good choice exceeding my expectations'. **Saman Ahsani, 31 (Iran)**

NB:STUDIO
Insead
MBA Program

Art Directors:
Nick Finney, Ben Stott,
Alan Dye
Designer:
Daniel Lock
Client:
Insead

One year to earn
your place among
our alumni.

In a sense, you never leave INSEAD. As your MBA programme comes to an end, your life as an INSEAD alumnus begins. It is likely to be an unwitting, exciting life. You will join a diverse alumni network of around 32,300 members, 15,300 from the MBA programme and 16,900 from Executive programmes.

Our alumni live and work in over 150 countries across all continents. They may be geographically diverse, but they share the same entrepreneurial streak. Twenty years after gaining their MBA, over 40% of our alumni own and manage their own business. The advice and encouragement that flows between INSEAD alumni is an important tool in the business-building.

You may well wish to remain in touch with INSEAD. A thousand alumni volunteers sit on national alumni association committees, helping to organise reunions and international speaking events as well as interviewing MBA candidates in their home countries. The two alumni share their views here.

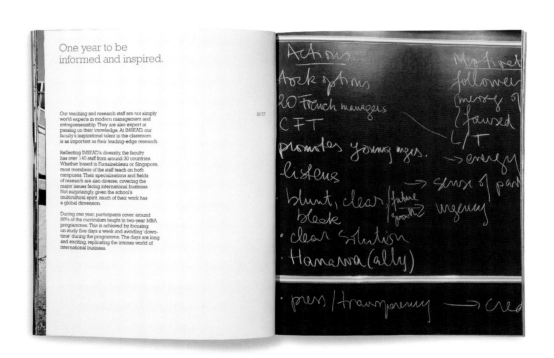

One year to be
informed and inspired.

Our teaching and research staff are not simply world experts in modern management and entrepreneurship. They are also expert at passing on their knowledge. At INSEAD, our faculty's inspirational talent in the classroom is as important as their leading-edge research.

Reflecting INSEAD's diversity, the faculty has over 140 staff from around 30 countries. Whether based in Fontainebleau or Singapore, most members of the staff teach on both campuses. Their specialisations and fields of research are also diverse, covering the major issues facing international business. Not surprisingly, given the school's multicultural spirit, much of their work has a global dimension.

During one year, participants cover around 80% of the curriculum taught in two-year MBA programmes. This is achieved by focusing on study five days a week and avoiding 'down-time' during the programme. The days are long and exciting, replicating the intense world of international business.

Building the Jubilee School
Everyone and the Architect

Building Sights
Building Sights is a campaign to involve the public in building projects. Run by Arts Council England and the Commission for Architecture and the Built Environment (CABE), Building Sights is an award scheme to celebrate the best examples of public involvement and a website that provides practical information and ideas about how to go about it.

This book is the story of a new school in Tulse Hill, Brixton, London. It comes in two parts;

Part One
How the process was shared

Part Two
How the school was designed

Awards for the school

Aug 2001
RSA Art for Architecture Award

Aug 2003
RIBA Regional Award

Sept 2003
Short-listed for the Prime Minister's Better Public Building Award

Sept 2003
Short-listed for a Building Construction Industry Award

Part One
A guide to sharing the process – getting everyone involved in the process of creating a new building.

STUDIO
MYERSCOUGH
Jubilee

Art Director:
Morag Myerscough
Designers:
Morag Myerscough,
David Lowbridge
Client:
Arts Council England,
CABE & Allford, Hall,
Monaghan, Morris

SELF-
PROMOTIONAL
BROCHURES

DESIGN FIRM > Graif Design
ART DIRECTOR > Matt Graif
DESIGNER > Matt Graif
CLIENT > Seven Course Design
TOOLS (SOFTWARE/PLATFORM) > Illustrator 9.0
PAPER STOCK > Neenah Paper Co.
PRINTING PROCESS > Offset printing

DESIGN FIRM › Fork Unstable Media GMBH
ART DIRECTOR › David Linderman
DESIGNER › David Linderman
COPYWRITER › David Linderman
CLIENT › Fork Unstable Media
TOOLS (SOFTWARE/PLATFORM) › Freehand 8.0, Photoshop 5.5, Capture v 4.0, Macintosh platform
PAPER STOCK › Gmund "Havanna," Munken "Munken Pur"
PRINTING PROCESS › Three-color, U.V. glaze

DESIGN FIRM > Pepe Gimeno - Proyecto Gráfico
ART DIRECTOR > Pepe Gimeno
DESIGNERS > Suso Pérez, José P. Gill
CLIENT > Pepe Gimeno - Proyecto Gráfico
TOOLS (SOFTWARE/PLATFORM) > Freehand 8.0, Photosh
PRINTING PROCESS > Offset

Omaha Steaks is known as a premium purveyor and marketer of steaks, meats, and other gourmet foods. The Company sells its products internationally through a direct-mail catalog, retail stores, and the World Wide Web.

DESIGN FIRM > Fitch
ART DIRECTOR > Mark Uskavich
DESIGNER > Mark Uskavich
ILLUSTRATOR/PHOTOGRAPHER > Mark Uskavich
CLIENT > Fitch
PRINTING PROCESS > Baesman Printing

DESIGN FIRM > Foco Media gmbh & cte
ART DIRECTOR > Steffen Janus
DESIGNER > Steffen Janus
CLIENT > Foco Media gmbh & cte

DESIGN FIRM › Oh Boy, A Design Company
ART DIRECTOR › David Salanitro
DESIGNERS › Hunter Wimmer, Ted Bluey
PHOTOGRAPHER › Hunter Wimmer
COPYWRITERS › David Salanitro, Hunter Wimmer
CLIENT › Oh Boy, A Design Company
PAPER STOCK › Mohawk 65 lb. superfine, ultrawhite
PRINTING PROCESS › Offset, sheet fed

Microsoft: Hermes Internet Telephone
The future of communications

NASA spent $200 million on computers to put a man on the moon. Today the same technology costs $900.

In a world of technology overload, consumers are looking for products that do fewer things better

FITCH! BUSINESS SUCCESS BY DESIGN

DESIGN FIRM > Fitch
ART DIRECTOR > Vassoula Vasiliou
DESIGNER > Kian Kuan
CLIENT > Fitch

DESIGN FIRM > Louey/Rubino Design Group Inc.
ART DIRECTOR > Robert Louey
DESIGNERS > Robert Louey, Alex Chao, Anja Mueller
ILLUSTRATORS/PHOTOGRAPHERS > Eric Tucker, Jamey Stillings, Everard Williams Jr., Lise Metzger,
Neal Brown, Ann Elliot Cutting, Hugh Kretschmer
COPYWRITER > Elisabeth Charney
CLIENT > Louey/Rubino Design Group
TOOLS (SOFTWARE/PLATFORM) > QuarkXPress, Macintosh
PAPER STOCK > Mead Signature dull, Gilbert Oxford

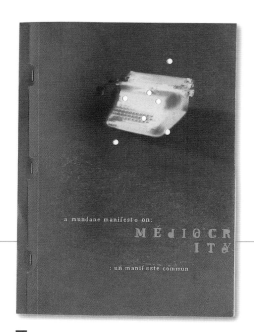

IRIDIUM, A DESIGN AGENCY
A MUNDANE MANIFESTO ON MEDIOCRITY

ART DIRECTORS:
JEAN-LUC DENAT
MARIO L'ÉCUYER

DESIGNER:
MARIO L'ÉCUYER

PHOTOGRAPHER:
HEADLIGHT
INNOVATIVE IMAGERY

CLIENT:
ROLLAND INC

SOFTWARE AND
HARDWARE:
ILLUSTRATOR
PHOTOSHOP
QUARKXPRESS
MAC G4

MATERIALS:
ROLLAND MOTIF

PRINTING:
LOMOR PRINTERS

CANADA

ELFEN
IN-HOUSE BROCHURE

ART DIRECTOR:
COMBINED

DESIGNERS:
GUTO EVANS
GWION PRYDDERCH
MATHEW JAMES

CLIENT:
ELFEN

SOFTWARE:
FREEHAND
PHOTOSHOP
QUARKXPRESS

MATERIALS:
CYCLUS OFFSET

PRINTING:
LITHO

www.elfen.co.uk

WALES

Beaten by Neo Nazis.
January in Minneapolis.
Stripped naked. Thrown
from bridge. I am dead.
Much later. Found.
Toe tagged. Placed in
morgue. Wake. See
tag. Scream. I am alive.

Michael Walter Johnson

The end.

I GET UP AT 5 IN THE MORN-
ING AND I DON'T HATE IT.
Twelve Chevy Suburbans and
twenty five years later Steve
still digs his job. Exclusive to
one company, an engineering
firm with clients spread across
the map. He's seen many jobs
inside and outside of his
company, proclaiming his the
best of all. Every day is different,
every day is still worthy of that
5 a.m. wake-up call.

BIG HIT AND RUN.
He gets the best of people.
All the personal interaction
he needs. Just enough, not
too much. Swing in for an
anniversary party, a birthday
party, have a slice of cake,
pizza, a handful of mixed
nuts and move on.

GREEN THUMBS ON THE
WHEEL.
A double lot in south
Minneapolis and a family
history in horticulture makes
Steve a favorite with the
ladies. Just watch 'em
beam as he slides in with
a gathering of fresh flowers
hand-selected from the
Bachleitner Gardens.

ANTIQUE ROAD SHOWMAN.
The secret life of Steve
Bachleitner—arranged and
running appraisal and estate
sales. Tagging the remains
and remnants of an existence
in dim attics and hat boxes
and stubborn drawers are the
letters, photographs and
props of lives lived and lost.
A skill possibly inherited from
his father, the candy, cigarette
and gum salesman, who
would drag his boys to
the dump and drag home
assorted unmemorable finds.
A collector in his own right,
he wants us all to watch
for the sale notice on the
Steve Bachleitner estate—
he guarantees it'll be a good
one. (Not too soon Steve,
we can wait.)

Steve Bachleitner
window on the world

I'M A HAPPY GUY
He's a happy guy.

GRAPHICULTURE
"DIRECT"—THE COURIER BOOK

DESIGNER:
BETH MUELLER

CLIENT:
GRAPHICULTURE

MATERIALS:
WAUSAU PAPERS

PRINTING:
LANDMARK COLOUR
COMMUNICATIONS

Bob Alexander

WILLOUGHBY DESIGN GROUP
THE ONLY CONSTANT IS CHANGE

WHAT ARE OUR GUIDING PRINCIPLES?
WHAT WILL NEVER CHANGE...

WHAT IS OUR REASON FOR COMING TO WORK EACH DAY?
WHAT IS THE SOUL OF OUR COMPANY?

our vision is...

WILLOUGHBY DESIGN GROUP

DEFINE

FUTURE PLANNING RETREAT 2002

ART DIRECTOR:	DESIGNER:	CLIENT:	SOFTWARE AND	MATERIALS:	PRINTING:
ANN WILLOUGHBY	TRENTON KENAGY	WILLOUGHBY DESIGN GROUP	HARDWARE: QUARKXPRESS MAC	OFFSET	IN-HOUSE

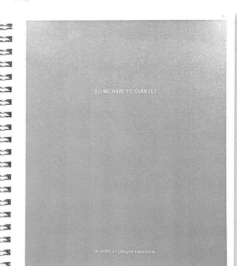

?

we have a great reputation, clients, people and work, so why?

DO WE HAVE TO CHANGE?

in order to prosper tomorrow

WILLOUGHBY DESIGN GROUP

FUTURE PLANNING RETREAT 2002

ART DIRECTOR:
NATALIE LAM

DESIGNER:
NATALIE LAM

CLIENT:
LEAD DOG DIGITAL

SOFTWARE:
ILLUSTRATOR
QUARKXPRESS

MATERIALS:
FRENCH

PRINTING:
SEIDEL

LEAD DOG DIGITAL
LEAD DOG DIGITAL BROCHURE

qué   cho   ema   esi

ART DIRECTOR: DESIGNER: CLIENT: SOFTWARE AND   PRINTING:
MIKE TEIXEIRA   MIKE TEIXEIRA   KOLÉGRAMDESIGN   HARDWARE: DU PROGRÈS
                                                                QUARKXPRESS   ALBION
                                                                MAC   LOMOR PRINTING

CANADA

PAULA KELLY DESIGN

Gallery Exhibit Catalog for Collection
of Vintage Salt and Pepper Shakers

ART DIRECTOR:	DESIGNER:	CLIENT:	TOOLS:	MATERIALS:
Paula Kelly	Paula Kelly	Greenwich House Pottery	Adobe Illustrator	Utopia Two
		Jane Hatsook Gallery	QuarkXPress	(cover and text)

GRETEMAN GROUP
Read & Reap

ART DIRECTOR:	DESIGNERS:	ILLUSTRATOR:	CLIENT:	TOOLS:
Sonia Greteman	James Strange	James Strange	Greteman Group	Macromedia Freehand
CREATIVE DIRECTOR:	Craig Tomson	COPYWRITERS:		
Sonia Greteman		Sonia Greteman		
		Raleigh Drennon		

Pavo rarus
[haruldane jõululind, huviline kirjatuviline]

RUTH HUIMERIND

The Retro-Flavour Christmas Booklet
of the Paper Company

ART DIRECTOR:	DESIGNER:	CLIENT:	TOOLS:	MATERIALS:
Ruth Huimerind	Jyri Loun	Map Eesti	Macromedia Freehand	Century Acquarello Stucco Gesso

BBK STUDIO

Pique Catalog

ART DIRECTORS:	DESIGNER:	CLIENT:	TOOLS:	MATERIALS:
Yang Kim	Michele Chartier	Pique	Adobe Photoshop	Monadnock Astrolight
Michele Chartier			Adobe Illustrator	Super smooth
			QuarkXPress	

GET THE IDEA?
THE NEXT TIME YOU ARE SPECIFYING A C

HANGAR 18 CREATIVE GROUP
Starbright Paper Brochure

DESIGNER:	CLIENT:	TOOLS:	MATERIALS:
Sean Carter	Unisource Paper	QuarkXPress	Starbright Paper

SAGMEISTER INC.
Zumtobel Annual Report

ART DIRECTOR	DESIGNERS	CLIENT	TOOLS	MATERIALS
Stefan Sagmeister	Stefan Sagmeister Matthias Ernstberger	Zumtobel	Adobe Photoshop QuarkXPress	Molded relief sculpture

DUFFY SINGAPORE

A Photographer's Self-Promotion Brochure

ART DIRECTOR:	DESIGNER:	CLIENT:	TOOLS:	MATERIALS:
Christoper Lee	Christoper Lee	Wizards of Light	Macromedia Freehand	Artcard
				Art Paper

TRACY DESIGN COMMUNICATIONS
DDM Morris Photography Promotional

ART DIRECTOR:
Jan Tracy

DESIGNERS:
Tony Magliano
Rachel Karaca

CLIENT:
David Morris

TOOLS:
Adobe Photoshop
Adobe Illustrator
QuarkXPress

VINE360

VINE360 Brochure

DESIGNER:	**CLIENT:**	**TOOLS:**	**MATERIALS:**
Joy MacDonald	VINE360	Adobe Photoshop Adobe Illustrator	5inch.com CD silver stardream inkjet cardstock for individual customization

Some pairs bring out the best in each other. When the synergy is right, they complement each other's strengths, offer timely support, and make everything better and more interesting. Without Tonto, the Lone Ranger would be just a masked man lost in his tracks. Without Rudolph, Santa would still be stranded at the North Pole. Without jelly, peanut butter would be that brown gunky stuff that sticks to the roof of your mouth. And where would printers be without designers? And vice versa. As the best in the business will

GREAT PAIRINGS

admit: Behind every great printer is a great designer, and behind every great designer is a great printer. That's the reason we have added a new Designer Awards component to the 2004 Sappi North America Printer of the Year program. A panel of nationally known designers will judge all design entries, with the top 18 winners showcased in a traveling exhibition and full-color show catalog. What's more, all 18 design winners (and a guest) will be honored at an all-expense paid gala celebration at a five-star resort this spring. But hurry, the entry deadline is January 15.

PENTAGRAM DESIGN/SF

Call for Entries

ART DIRECTOR:	DESIGNER:	CLIENT:	TOOLS:	MATERIALS:
Kit Hinrichs	Belle How	Sappi Fine Paper	Adobe Photoshop	McCoy Silk 100 lb (text)
			Adobe Illustrator	McCoy Gloss 100 lb (cover)
			QuarkXPress	

THING #5

Marketing Schizophrenia

"I want to be unique,"

one marketing manager told us, holding up his competitors' ad. "Just like them." A classic case of marketing schizophrenia.

The problem stems from two conflicting drives in the head of every business-to-business marketer.

The need to be unique. *Positioning, branding, the so-called USP—all of their marketing principles hinge on being different from everyone else.*

The need to be the same. *Credibility and security come from belonging to a group, from being like everyone else.*

Which need usually wins out? Guess. And the resulting advertising is just another anonymous penguin on the iceberg.

There is only one time when "me-too" is a smart strategy. When you aspire to be considered among a different category of players from the one you're associated with. In that case, go ahead, emulate the behavior of the desired group. Clients aboard their iceberg.

Then, once you're on, use advertising for what it's supposed to do. Differentiate you. Business reasons demand that you strive to be unique. Figure out what makes you distinctive and then use your advertising to celebrate the hell out of it.

THING #6

Trying Too Hard

That guy at the party with the lampshade on his head,

you're probably seen the ads he creates. They're so frantically determined to win your attention, they'll mesmerize you—for about a second and a half.

At eleven-point you'll realize you don't really get it or don't really care—and boldly turn the page.

Ads like these often rely on borrowed interest. Dogs, race cars and spokesmodels are popular. Our study turned up all three, plus a naked pregnant woman.

Then there are the ads that are simply too hard to decipher. Some we came across demanded we read the entire ad in order to grasp the creative concept that was supposed to get us to read the ad in the first place. Entirely self-defeating. Others were completely inscrutable. We're still wondering about the two guys riding the shopping cart across the banking software ad.

Saddest of all are the ads, some of which evince a spark of creativity, that are killed by their own hyperactive art directors. The murder weapons: Illegible type. Graphic gewgaws crammed into all available white space. A chaotic swirl of fonts and colors sure to suffocate any message that might have been there in the first place.

If you notice that ad instead of the message, it's standing in its own way.

Gewgaws. Actual examples of graphically gratuitous elements, excised from ads in our study.

THE DAVE AND ALEX SHOW
The Dave and Alex Show Broadside

ART DIRECTORS	DESIGNER	CLIENT	TOOLS	MATERIALS
Alex Isley	Dana Moran	The Dave and Alex Show	QuarkXPress	Newsprint
Dave Goldenberg				

Why do so many **business-to-business ads suck?**

A Broadside from The Dave and Alex Show

USINE DE BOUTONS

Maya Runs

ART DIRECTOR:	DESIGNERS:	CLIENT:	TOOLS:
Chiara Grandesso	Chiara Grandesso	USINE de BOUTONS	Adobe Illustrator
	Lionello Borean		

TRACY DESIGN COMMUNICATIONS
DDM Morris Photography Promotional

ART DIRECTOR:	DESIGNERS:	CLIENT:	TOOLS:
Jan Tracy	Tony Magliano	David Morris	Adobe Photoshop
	Rachel Karaca		Adobe Illustrator
			QuarkXPress

DOPPIO DESIGN

Self-Promotional Piece

ART DIRECTOR:	DESIGNERS:	CLIENT:	TOOLS:	MATERIALS:
Mauro Bertolini	Amber Kadwell	Doppio Design	Adobe Photoshop	Medley Satin Uncoated
	Mauro Bertolini		Adobe Illustrator	100 gsm

BAUMANN & BAUMANN
A Twenty-Six-Letter Book

ART DIRECTOR:	DESIGNERS:	CLIENT:	TOOLS:
Barbara Baumann	Barbara Baumann	Hatje Cantz, Ostfildern	Macromedia Freehand
Gerd Baumann	Gerd Baumann		

HIPPO STUDIO
FCS Company Brochure

ART DIRECTORS:	DESIGNERS:	CLIENT:	TOOLS:	MATERIALS:
William Ho Siu Chuen	William Ho Siu Chuen	FCS Limited	Adobe Photoshop	Curious Metallics Metal
Chin Lee Ma	Chin Lee Ma		Adobe Illustrator	Ionished Antique cover
	Stone Lam			

FLIGHT CREATIVE
Flight Creative Promotional Brochure

ART DIRECTOR:
Lisa Nankervis

DESIGNERS:
Lisa Nankervis
Alex Fregon
David Stelma

CLIENT:
Flight Creative

TOOLS:
Adobe Illustrator
3D Studio Max

MATERIALS:
Sumo 250 gsm
Central Die-cut Slit

Ó! GRAFÍSK HÖNNUN

Ó!
Self-Promotion

ART DIRECTOR:	DESIGNER:	CLIENT:	TOOLS:	MATERIALS:
Einar Gylfason	Einar Gylfason	Ó!	Macromedia Freehand	Munken Lynx

BLACKLETTER DESIGN INC

Self-Promotion Brochure/Book for Illustrator

ART DIRECTORS:	DESIGNER:	CLIENT:	TOOLS:	MATERIALS:
Ken Bessie	Ken Bessie	Rick Sealock	Adobe Illustrator	Stora Enso Paper Centura
Rick Sealock			QuarkXPress	

ALLEGRO 168
**12th Anniversary
Carnival Invitation**

Art Directors:
Nicole Vallée,
Mario L'Écuyer
Designer:
Mario L'Écuyer
Client:
Allegro 168
Software:
QuarkXPress,
Adobe Illustrator,
Adobe Photoshop
Paper/Materials:
Fraser Papers
Pegasus, Kraft
paper bags, custom
rubber stamp

HAT-TRICK DESIGN
How Do You Do?
Self-Promotional
Brochure

Art Directors:
Jim Sutherland,
Gareth Howat,
David Kimpton
Designers:
Jim Sutherland,
Adam Giles,
Ben Christie
Client:
Hat-Trick Design
Software:
QuarkXPress
Paper/Materials:
Astralux, Lite Gloss,
Hanno Gloss

The 'N' becomes a window into a myriad of images that demonstrate the diversity, brightness, excitement and scale of the natural world.

Under the new identity, there is no doubt that anything produced by the Natural History Museum signifies a distinct and powerful experience, courtesy of a distinct and powerful source: nature itself.

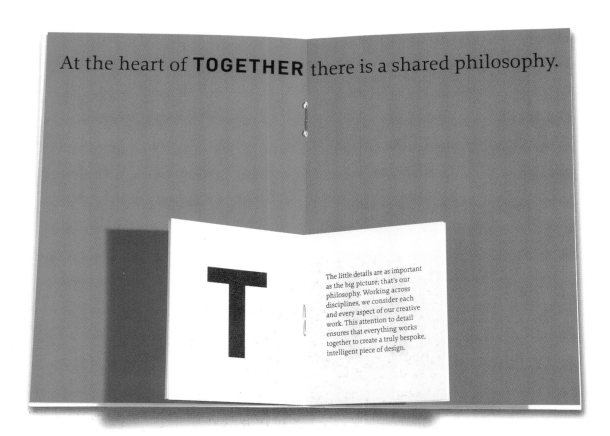

At the heart of **TOGETHER** there is a shared philosophy.

The little details are as important as the big picture; that's our philosophy. Working across disciplines, we consider each and every aspect of our creative work. This attention to detail ensures that everything works together to create a truly bespoke, intelligent piece of design.

TOGETHER DESIGN
Self-Promotional Brochure

Designers:
Katja Thielen,
Heidi Lightfoot
Client:
Together Design
Software:
QuarkXPress
Paper/Materials:
Conqueror Wove,
Metallic Foil Block

TOGETHER

GALLERY
of COSTUME
& TEXTILES

WE LIKE BEAUTIFUL THINGS

When Kyra Segal approached us with a view to creating an identity for her eponymous clothing collection, we jumped at the chance. Beautifully designed and impeccably crafted, her pieces are inspired by the timeless aesthetics and craftsmanship of the archives at The Gallery of Costume and Textiles, the famous emporium of antique textiles and vintage clothes founded by Kyra's father Lionel. Our challenge was to create an identity to be applied across the retail environment, which would tell the story of the collection's provenance and aesthetics, yet stand alone as a modern, covetable brand.

We found inspiration for the identity in the phoenix, a symbol of resurrection, good luck, and a theme of great personal resonance to Kyra herself. Depicted in an antique, chinoiserie style, the identity ultimately reflects the eclectic nature of the Gallery and of Kyra's own aesthetic, as well as being a beautiful thing in itself.

WE LIKE FINDING REASONS TO CELEBRATE

Which is why we were only too keen to work on a project which would set the corks a-popping on a regular basis. Katja from Together comes from a wine-making family in the Mosel valley, and the time was right to introduce their wines to the UK market. With no retail presence and a largely word-of-mouth approach to marketing, they needed a website to support their all-important ordering system, as well as a redesigned logo for bottle labels, tags, postcards and wine corks.

We developed a new logo and commissioned illustrations which became the backbone of the website. Taking the form of a conversation, the site features both real and fictitious characters taking the visitor on a tour of the Thielen wine cellar, and engagingly holding forth about the wines, and the history, philosophy and techniques behind them. The creative work has a look, feel and tone which is refreshingly different and unique, which may reflect the fact that most of the contributors were paid in wine, a good deal of it in advance, for inspiration's sake. www.thielenwine.com

ARTS,
ENTERTAINMENT,
AND EVENT
BROCHURES

DESIGN FIRM › Bolt
ART DIRECTORS › Jamey Boiter, Mark Thwaites, Deanna Mancuso
DESIGNERS › Jamey Boiter, Mark Thwaites, Deanna Mancuso
ILLUSTRATOR/PHOTOGRAPHER › Stephanie Chesson
COPYWRITERS › IDSA & Bolt
CLIENT › IDSA
TOOLS (SOFTWARE/PLATFORM) › Photoshop, Illustrator, QuarkXPress
PRINTING PROCESS › 4-color, spot metallic

DESIGN FIRM > Trickett & Webb Ltd.
DESIGNERS > Lynn Trickett, Brian Webb, Katja Thielen
PHOTOGRAPHER > Adam Mitchinson
CLIENT > The London Institute
TOOLS (SOFTWARE/PLATFORM) > QuarkXPress
PAPER STOCK > Munken Lynx and Parilux
PRINTING PROCESS > Four-color lithography

DESIGN FIRM › Sayles Graphic
ART DIRECTOR › John Sayles
DESIGNER › John Sayles
ILLUSTRATOR › John Sayles
CLIENT › Pattee Enterprises
TOOLS (SOFTWARE/PLATFORM)
PRINTING PROCESS › Offset

DESIGN FIRM > Lowercase, Inc.
ART DIRECTOR > Tim Bruce
DESIGNER > Tim Bruce
ILLUSTRATOR/PHOTOGRAPHER > Tim Bruce
CLIENT > Writers' Theatre Chicago
TOOLS (SOFTWARE/PLATFORM) > QuarkXPress, Macintosh
PAPER STOCK > Cougar

DESIGN FIRM > INOX Design, Milan
ART DIRECTORS > Claudio Gavazzi, Sabrina Elena
DESIGNERS > Claudio Gavazzi, Sabrina Elena
COPYWRITER > Michela Sartorio
CLIENT > MTV Networks
TOOLS (SOFTWARE/PLATFORM) > QuarkXPress, Photoshop
PAPER STOCK/PRINTING PROCESS > Opaque coated paper
PRINTING PROCESS > Four-color offset, gloss varnish

DESIGN FIRM > LA Weekly
ART DIRECTOR > Sheryl Scott
DESIGNER > Sheryl Scott
CLIENT > LA Weekly Music Awards
TOOLS (SOFTWARE/PLATFORM) > QuarkXPress, Photoshop

DESIGNER:
DAPHNE DIAMANT
PATRICK DEVLIN

PHOTOGRAPHER:
RANKIN

CLIENT:
WORLD SNOOKER

SOFTWARE AND
HARDWARE:
ILLUSTRATOR
PHOTOSHOP
QUARKXPRESS
MAC

MATERIALS:
MEDLEY AND PVC
PACK

PRINTING:
MIDAS

UK

USA

1999 design awards
society for environmental graphic design

POULIN + MORRIS
SEGD

DESIGNERS:
L. RICHARD POULIN
DOUGLAS MORRIS

CLIENT:
SOCIETY FOR
ENVIRONMENTAL
GRAPHIC DESIGN

SOFTWARE:
QUARKXPRESS

MATERIALS:
SAPPI LUSTRO

PRINTING:
QUALITY PRINTING

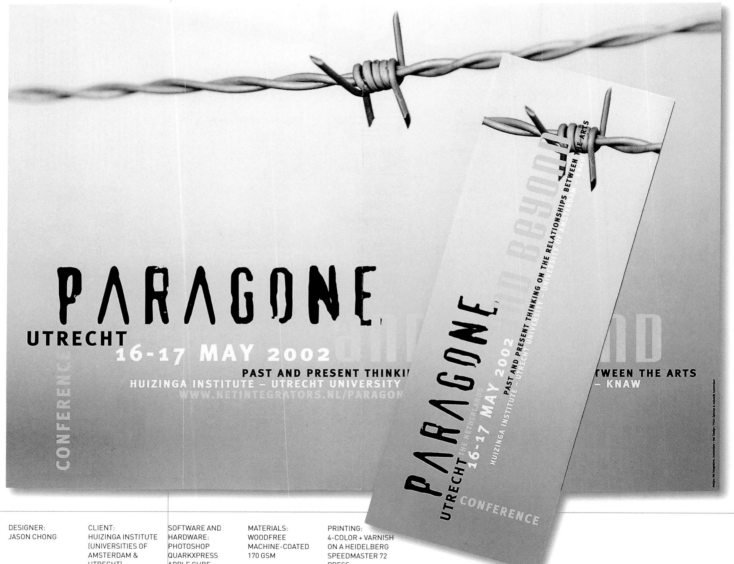

ART DIRECTOR:
JASON CHONG

DESIGNER:
JASON CHONG

CLIENT:
HUIZINGA INSTITUTE
(UNIVERSITIES OF
AMSTERDAM &
UTRECHT)

SOFTWARE AND
HARDWARE:
PHOTOSHOP
QUARKXPRESS
APPLE CUBE
PC

MATERIALS:
WOODFREE
MACHINE-COATED
170 GSM

PRINTING:
4-COLOR + VARNISH
ON A HEIDELBERG
SPEEDMASTER 72
PRESS

NET INTEGRATORS – NET DESIGN
CONFERENCE POSTER/FLYER/PROGRAM
(PRO BONO)

ART DIRECTOR:
ANNIE LACHAPELLE

DESIGNER:
ANNIE LACHAPELLE

CLIENT:
CINÉMATHÈQUE
QUÉBÉCOISE

SOFTWARE:
ILLUSTRATOR
PHOTOSHOP
QUARKXPRESS

CANADA

KO CREATION
LA REVUE

FABIO ONGARATO DESIGN
LINEAGE: THE ARCHITECTURE OF
DANIEL LIBESKIND

AUSTRALIA

ART DIRECTOR: FABIO ONGARATO	DESIGNER: JAMES LIN	CLIENT: JEWISH MUSEUM OF AUSTRALIA	MATERIALS: NORDSET	PRINTING: GUNN & TAYLOR

07
POINT, LIFE,
LINE

ART DIRECTOR:
DANIEL BASTIAN

DESIGNERS:
DANIEL BASTIAN
MAYA DA SILVA
JUTTA HOFFMANN

PHOTOGRAPHER:
TOM KLEINER

CLIENT:
DESIGN ZENTRUM
BREMEN

SOFTWARE:
PHOTOSHOP
QUARKXPRESS

MATERIALS:
ZANDERS MEGA
MATT 135 OFFSET

PRINTING:
FRANKE DRUCK

büro 7

gruppe für gestaltung

Das Gestaltungsbüro entwickelt und realisiert seit 1993 umfassende Kommunikationskonzepte zur Umsetzung marktgerechter Unternehmensstrategien. Auf der Basis von fundierten Analysen werden Lösungen erarbeitet, die die Unternehmensidentität des Kunden nach innen und außen effektiv kommunizieren.

Büro 7, Telefon 0421-7 37 07

14 Gestalter unterschiedlicher Fachrichtungen arbeiten in den Bereichen Werbung, Grafik, Interieurdesign und Möbelgestaltung. Diese Zusammenarbeit unterschiedlicher Disziplinen führt zu ganzheitlichen Gestaltungslösungen.

Gruppe für Gestaltung, Telefon 0421-33 86 80

GERMANY

er

bremer gestalten

Eine Ausstellung im Design Zentrum Bremen

Künstler x Bremer Design

josef hattig

Mein Haus versteht Designförderung immer als Wirtschaftsförderung und auch als Hilfe zur Selbsthilfe. Sie soll sowohl die Innovationskraft von Unternehmen stärken als auch das im Bundesland Bremen vorhandene kreative Potential sichtbar machen und mehren.

Das Design Zentrum Bremen hat daher eine Ausstellungsserie begonnen, in der die Vielfalt kreativer Dienstleistungen im Designbereich am Beispiel vorwiegend kleinerer und jüngerer Designbüros gezeigt wird.

Wir hoffen, daß bereits die erste Ausstellung dieser Reihe vielen mittelständischen Unternehmen, aber auch Existenzgründern den Anstoß gibt, Design in ihre Unternehmensstrategie einzubeziehen.

Der Ausstellung, die im Rahmen von „Advantage: Design" der Design-Initiative der deutschen Wirtschaft stattfindet, wünsche ich einen großen Erfolg, zahlreiche Kontakte zwischen Unternehmern und Designern und viel öffentliche Resonanz.

Josef Hattig
Senator für Wirtschaft, Mittelstand, Technologie und Europaangelegenheiten

FORM5 + BÜRO7
BREMERGESTALTEN

renate wedepohl

Schmuck zum Gernetragen. Egal ob zum Alltagskleid oder zum kleinen Schwarzen, die Kollektionen der Schmuckdesignerin verleihen jedem Outfit den letzten Schliff. Ausgewogene Proportionen und klassische Materialien bestimmen das charakteristische Erscheinungsbild ihrer Werke. Schlichtes Silber, üppiges Gold und kühles Platin stehen sich oft komplementär gegenüber und erzeugen einen spannungsreichen Kontrast zwischen strenger Geometrie und verspielten Ornamenten.

Renate Wedepohl, Telefon 0421-70 39 22

lina namuth

Seit 1984 entwirft die Künstlerin in ihrer eigenen Werkstatt Damen- und Herren-Oberbekleidung aus hochwertigen und originellen Stoffen. Jedes Stück erscheint als Unikat oder im Rahmen einer Kleinserie, was dem Kunden große Individualität garantiert. „Mein Ziel ist es, Kleidung zu entwickeln, die das Leben angenehm macht, die Patina ansetzen darf wie ein gutes Möbelstück, in der man alles tun kann." Die Mode von Lina Namuth ist schlicht, bequem, elegant und einfach zu tragen.

Lina Namuth, Telefon 0421-32 63 66

USINE DE BOUTONS
MALOFANCON PRESS BROCHURE

ITALY

malofancon
PRESS RELEASE

ART DIRECTORS: DESIGNERS: CLIENT: PRINTING:
LIONELLO BOREAN   LIONELLO BOREAN   MALOFANCON   CMYK + 1 PANTONE
CHIARA GRANDESSO   CHIARA GRANDESSO   FURNITURE

5453

SOME TRAINS IN AMERICA

ART DIRECTOR:
VINCE FROST

DESIGNER:
VINCE FROST

PHOTOGRAPHER:
ANDREW CROSS

CLIENT:
CHRIST BOOT/
PRESTEL

MATERIALS:
EURO ART SILK
170GSM

PRINTING:
EBS. ITALY

UK

0006: SOUTHERN CALIFORNIA 0030: TEXAS 0040: APPALACHIA 0062: NORTHEAST   0088: MIDWEST 0114: NORTHWEST 0140: CENTRAL CALIFORNIA

FROST DESIGN
SOME TRAINS IN AMERICA

0088

SOME TRAINS IN AMERICA: MIDWEST

>IROQUOIS OCT 1L 2001

ART DIRECTOR:
PING-PONG DESIGN

DESIGNER:
PING-PONG DESIGN

ILLUSTRATOR:
PING-PONG DESIGN
LUUK BODE
CIRQUE DE PEPIN
HANS VAN BENTEM
DJ CHANTELLE

CLIENT:
MAM SHOWROOM
FOR MEDIA AND
MOVING ART

SOFTWARE:
ILLUSTRATOR
PHOTOSHOP
QUARKXPRESS

MATERIALS:
REVIVA OFFSET
POLAR SUPER
GESATINEERD

PRINTING:
OFFSET

PING-PONG DESIGN
ARTOONISM

AUSTRALIA

ART DIRECTOR:
FABIO ONGARATO

DESIGNER:
JAMES LIN

CLIENT:
KAREN WALKER

MATERIALS:
SILK GLOSS

PRINTING:
ENERGI

FABIO ONGARATO DESIGN
KAREN WALKER WINTER 2001

HATCH CREATIVE
BODYTORQUE

ART DIRECTOR:	DESIGNER:	PHOTOGRAPHER:	CLIENT:	SOFTWARE:	MATERIALS:	PRINTING:
SASKIA ERICSON	SASKIA ERICSON	LOIS GREENFIELD	THE AUSTRALIAN BALLET	ILLUSTRATOR PHOTOSHOP STREAMLINE	GILCLEAR OXFORD GILBERT PAPER	4-COLOR PROCESS BAMBRA PRESS

Australian Ballet dancers have a distinctive style of dance that has been talked about for as long as the company has been in existence; a formidable technique combined with a daring attitude. **bodytorque** gets you up-close and personal with some of Australia's most dynamic contemporary artists.

"A buncha cowgirls on pointe, so fearless" William Forsythe

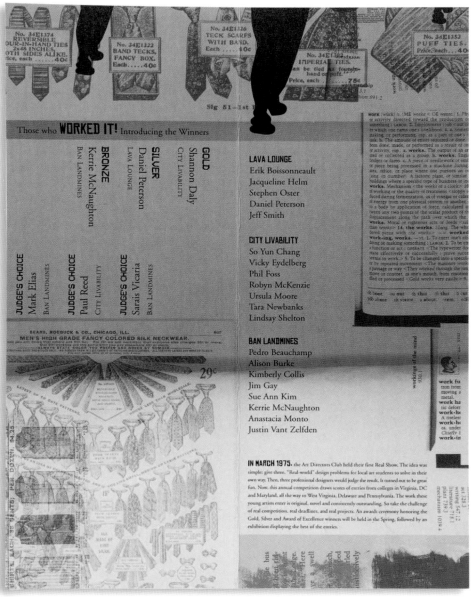

FUSZION COLLABORATIVE

Real Show Reception

ART DIRECTOR:
John Foster

DESIGNER:
John Foster

CLIENT:
ADCMW

TOOLS:
Adobe Photoshop
Adobe Illustrator
QuarkXPress

MATERIALS:
Domtar Titanium

Marcia Breece + Kasey Demonstrates Centrifugal Force + Photograph

TRANSMOGRIFY

Mark Monlux + Atomic Toaster + Vector

GREENZWEIG DESIGN

Art Jam 6—Buyers Invitation

ART DIRECTOR:	DESIGNER:	CLIENT:	TOOLS:
Tim Greenzweig	Tim Greenzweig	Graphic Artists Guild	Adobe Photoshop
		Seattle	QuarkXPress

EXPERIENCE THE LATEST IN ALTERNATIVE ENERGY

ART JAM 6

ENERGIZE

John Terence Turner + Windfarm + Photograph

Shane L. Johnson + Creative Matter + Adobe Illustrator

ELFEN

Craft Catalogue

ART DIRECTOR:	DESIGNER:	CLIENT:	TOOLS:	MATERIALS:
Guto Evans	Matthew James	Wales Arts International	Macromedia Freehand QuarkXPress	Curtis Echo Artik matt

THE RUSSO-JAPANESE WAR

During the Russo-Japanese War (1904–5), more than one million Japanese soldiers fought Russian troops for control of Korea and Manchuria. Postcards—which from the beginning had been used for documentation, memorialization, and propaganda—were particularly relevant in wartime and became the preferred way for families to maintain contact with the armed forces and follow the progress of the war. The Japanese government issued five sets of postcards with scenes of battles, courageous soldiers, and victory celebrations. The demand for these was so great that between 400,000 and 700,000

individual cards were issued. In addition, approximately one thousand sets of privately printed postcards (forty-five hundred different designs) fed the frenzy, and by the time the war was over, an estimated four thousand postcard outlets existed in Tokyo alone.

Among the privately printed postcards is an image, extending across three cards, with a sinking Russian ship juxtaposed against a stylized map of Japan (fig. 2). The inscription along the bottom edge notes that the cards were designed for a competition, presumably in commemoration of Japan's victory.

On June 1, 1906, the government issued its last set of postcards, celebrating the Japanese victory. This set included a photographic image documenting thousands of people waiting in line to buy these postcards (see page 15, fig. 12). At top and lower right of the card are lithographs showing customers completing their purchases and an official providing commemorative stamps. One observer noted: "When unsuccessful buyers were given a notice that all cards had gone, they stormed the office and smashed window panes."

fig. 2
Commemorating the Great Naval Battle of the Japan Sea (detail), late Meiji era, canceled, 1906

NEW YEAR'S POSTCARDS

The exchange of greetings at New Year's—traditionally in the form of personal visits—has been a revered custom in Japan since ancient times. When the mail system was established, however, the increasingly popular postcard became the favorite way to send good wishes to friends and relatives. It has been estimated that in 1905, for example, more than one hundred million postcards were sent to commemorate the New Year.

Many New Year's cards feature the twelve animals of the East Asian zodiac, which originated in China but has been known in Japan for almost two thousand years. The animals are placed in a traditional order to count the years. The years of the goat (fig. 9), for example, are 1907, 1919, 1931, and so on, up to 2003.

fig. 9 Takahashi Haruko (dates unknown), *New Year's Card: Goat, Shōwa era, 1931*

Atsuo (dates unknown), *New Year's Card: Women in Au Courant Fashion with Cityscape, Taishō–early Shōwa era* fig. 10

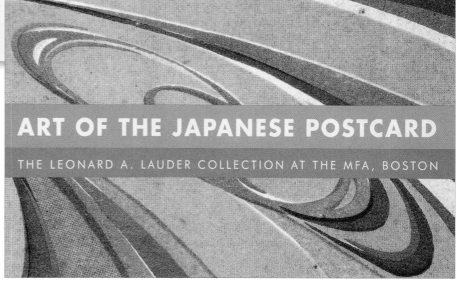

ART OF THE JAPANESE POSTCARD

THE LEONARD A. LAUDER COLLECTION AT THE MFA, BOSTON

MUSEUM OF FINE ARTS, BOSTON
Japanese Postcard Exhibit Brochure

ART DIRECTOR:	DESIGNER:	CLIENT:	TOOLS:	MATERIALS:
Janet O'Donoghue	Melissa Wehrman	Museum of Fine Arts Boston	Adobe Photoshop QuarkXPress	Monadnock Astrolite Silk Text 100 lb

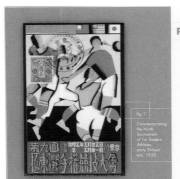

POSTCARDS AS ADVERTISEMENTS

Early Japanese advertising postcards primarily featured photographs, but designers soon enriched these photographs with lively, swirling borders influenced by Art Nouveau. After 1914, advertising design entered a new era, in which many styles of modern art were employed by artists who decided to become graphic designers rather than painters (fig. 7). Due to mechanical forms of reproduction and an increasing valuation of technology, graphic design—which created multiples for mass consumption, rather than unique objects for the individual—became a field in its own right.

Sugiura Hisui was a central figure in gaining recognition for graphic design as

a legitimate artistic pursuit. Working in an eclectic, East/West style, Hisui produced posters, brochures, magazine illustrations, and postcards for a number of companies, including the department store Mitsukoshi (fig. 8).

Founded as a dry-goods store in central Edo, Mitsukoshi (still operating today) flourished with Japan's economy and soon had branches throughout the country and elsewhere in Asia, hiring consultants who had studied American department-store management. Mitsukoshi introduced glass display cases and show windows and installed the country's first escalator in the main store. Mitsukoshi ultimately hired women as salesclerks, a job previously held only by men in Japan. In another radical departure from tradition, the store no longer required shoppers to leave their shoes at the entrance of the store.

fig. 7
Commemorating the Ninth Tournament of Far Eastern Athletes, early Shōwa era, 1930

fig. 8
Sugiura Hisui (1876–1965), *Commemorating the New Building of Mitsukoshi Department Store in Osaka, late Meiji era*

ROSE
**The Flower
Cabinet Exhibition
Catalog**

Art Director:
Simon Elliott
Designer:
Terry Stephens
Client:
Barbara and
Zafer Baran
Software:
QuarkXPress,
Adobe Photoshop
Paper/Materials:
Consort Royal Satin
250 gsm, Fenner
Redeem 70 gsm

The RSA Lecture Programme
For well over a century, the RSA has been organising lectures around the country to stimulate new thinking and fresh ideas about the challenges facing society. Not only do we attract the best speakers and attack the most diverse range of subjects, but we also promise a balanced and interactive debate.

Visit www.theRSA.org/events to see a complete listing of all RSA events, to listen to a lecture online or to book yourself a place on a forthcoming lecture.

Events include:

Lisa Jardine, Professor of History, Queen Mary and Westfield College – Ingenuity and Overstated

Panel discussion on Motion and Technology

Richard Kwiatkowski, United Nations Conference on Trade & Development

RSA at the Cheltenham Science Festival

"The sort of work the RSA does is broad, expansive... one of the few places that fosters genuine debate."

Quintin Ahlqvist, Presenter and Director, Servadini Blair

"When people with expertise in different areas talk to each other, everyone's a winner."

Alex James, Bass player, Blur

www.theRSA.org
Have you visited www.theRSA.org yet? It's the RSA's home on the web, a place that combines the quality of experience Fellows enjoy when visiting the John Adam Street House, with the interactive capabilities that make the web such a vibrant and important means of communication. Fellows who register can enter information about themselves – and seek other Fellows – in an online Directory; join in discussions in the informal but business-like Forum; and book seats for most RSA lectures. Of course, the usual news, in-depth reading material and general information are all available at the click of your mouse.

RSA Projects
The RSA delivers its mission through a portfolio of interdisciplinary projects, whose current aim is the advancement of a society keen on creativity and its principled exploitation. In particular the Programme aims to encourage innovation and invention; to help both the technology and the arts-based industries, to improve the national competence (knowledge, skills and behaviours); and to improve and extend professional standards.

The Society supports this activity by obtaining sponsorship from a diverse range of sources. Important among these is the expertise, effort and financial contribution of its Fellows. For more information, visit www.theRSA.org/projects

Project 1
Can the professions survive? – professional values for the 21st century
There is a widespread perception that the professions are under threat. No longer able to claim special privileges as disinterested, altruistic occupational groups acting detachedly in the public interest, professions are finding their traditional values and loyalties eroded.

In this climate, can – and should – the professions survive?

We are establishing a new project that seeks to consider some of these issues. The overall aim of the project is to re-invigorate the concept of a 'profession', to enlarge its application and to encourage the professions in the UK to become a more significant, trusted, and creative force for economic and social good.

The Comino Foundation has contributed towards the costs of this project.

Project 2
Science, Citizenship and the Market
This project is a major element of the RSA's move to strengthen its interventions in manufactures and commerce. All industry depends on a continuing flow of new science to maintain its product and process base but, as the recent GM controversy made clear, science-based industries ignore public opinion and perception at their peril. The failure to anticipate public reactions to a new technology can be expensive and damaging both for companies and for society.

We have made a significant investment to establish a project that will investigate the ways in which companies can benefit from incorporating socially sensitive antennae into their decision-making framework. One of the strengths of the project will lie in the collaboration between the RSA and a leading university: the project is being developed by the Science and Technology Studies Department of University College, London.

Project 3
The Economy of the Imagination
'The Economy of the Imagination' project, inspired by the New Statesman Lecture given by Lord Evans of the same title, aims to "find the line where high culture and commerce can meet to mutual advantage," as he put it. By examining each arts-based industry in turn, we will identify risk-takers who shun the easy temptation to produce formulaic, market-oriented products and support more innovative works. It is this risk-taking that we want to encourage.

www.theRSA.org/projects

NB:STUDIO
RSA New Members Handbook

Art Directors:
Nick Finney, Ben Stott, Alan Dye
Designers:
Nick Vincent, Tom Gauld
Client:
RSA

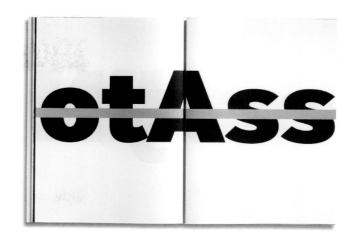

LIPPA PEARCE
**Circular 12,
Issue 12**

Art Director:
Domenic Lippa
Designer:
Domenic Lippa
Client:
The Typographic
Circle

SAGMEISTER INC.
**The Guggenheim,
Douglas Gordon**

Art Director:
Stefan Sagmeister
Designer:
Matthias Ernstberger
Typography:
Marian Bantjes
Production:
Lara Fieldbinder,
Melissa Secundino
Writer:
Nancy Spector
Client:
The Guggenheim
Museum, Berlin
Software:
Adobe CS
Paper/Materials:
Postcards

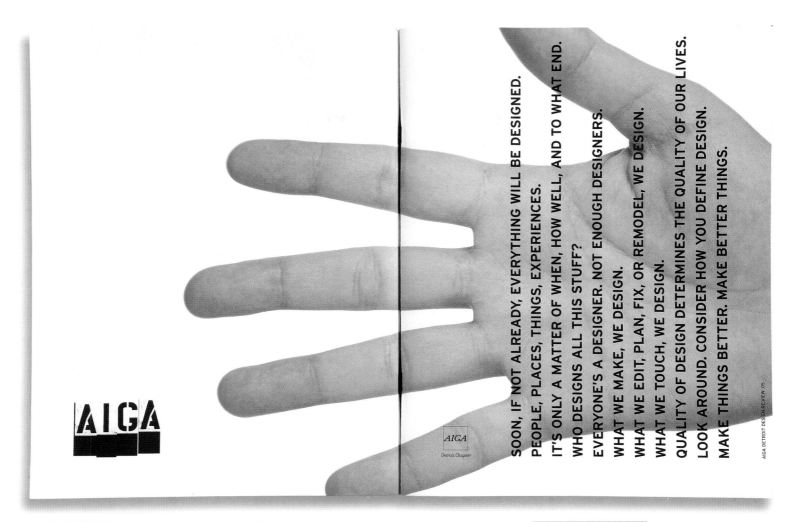

SOON, IF NOT ALREADY, EVERYTHING WILL BE DESIGNED.
PEOPLE, PLACES, THINGS, EXPERIENCES.
IT'S ONLY A MATTER OF WHEN, HOW WELL, AND TO WHAT END.
WHO DESIGNS ALL THIS STUFF?
EVERYONE'S A DESIGNER. NOT ENOUGH DESIGNERS.
WHAT WE MAKE, WE DESIGN.
WHAT WE EDIT, PLAN, FIX, OR REMODEL, WE DESIGN.
WHAT WE TOUCH, WE DESIGN.
QUALITY OF DESIGN DETERMINES THE QUALITY OF OUR LIVES.
LOOK AROUND. CONSIDER HOW YOU DEFINE DESIGN.
MAKE THINGS BETTER. MAKE BETTER THINGS.

AIGA

AIGA Detroit Chapter

AIGA DETROIT DESIGN REVIEW /05

BBK STUDIO
**AIGA Detroit
Design Re:View
'05 Awards Book**

Art Director:
Kevin Budelmann
Designers:
Brian Hauch,
Jason Murray
Client:
AIGA Detroit
Software:
Adobe Illustrator,
Adobe Photoshop,
QuarkXPress

BILLY BLUE CREATIVE,
PRECINCT
**AGDA Awards
Invite to Sydney**

Art Directors:
Justin Smith,
Geordie McKenzie
Designers:
Justin Smith,
Geordie McKenzie
Client:
AGDA
Software:
Adobe Illustrator,
Adobe Photoshop,
QuarkXPress

BC, MH
JAMES LAMBERT
**Monika Sosnowska
Art Pack**

Designers:
Ben Chatfield,
Mark Hopkins,
James Lambert
Client:
Serpentine Gallery
Software:
Adobe Illustrator,
QuarkXPress
Paper/Materials:
Beer Mat Board

VIVA DOLAN
COMMUNICATIONS
& DESIGN INC.
Prospectus Brochure

Art Director:
Frank Viva
Designer:
Todd Temporate
Client:
The Interior
Design Show
Software:
QuarkXPress
Paper/Materials:
Knightkote Matte
80 lb text cover

Free

Festival guide
May 16 to 29 2005

**SITUATION
LEEDS:
CONTEMPO
ARTISTS AN
PUBLIC REAI
05 05**

01/41:
Festival projects

42/47:
Talks

48/50:
Future projects

51/60:
Related projects

DESIGN PROJECT
**Situation Leeds
Festival Guide**

Art Directors:
Andy Probert,
James Littlewood
Designers:
Andy Probert,
James Littlewood
Client:
Situation Leeds
Software:
QuarkXPress,
Freehand
Paper/Materials:
Kaskad Flamingo
Pink, Raflatac
Glossprint (Robert
Horne)

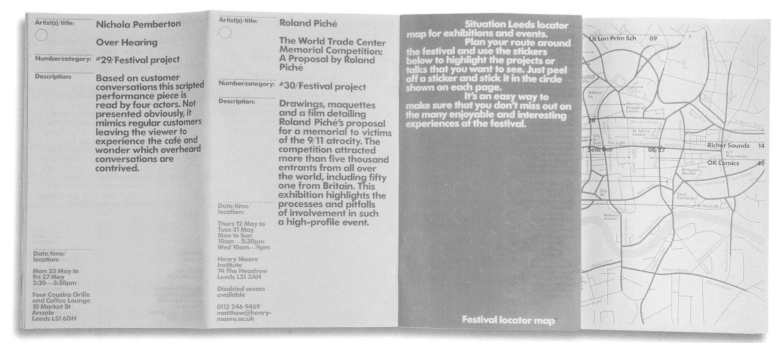

Artist(s)/title:	Nichola Pemberton
	Over Hearing
Number/category:	**#29/Festival project**
Description:	**Based on customer conversations this scripted performance piece is read by four actors. Not presented obviously, it mimics regular customers leaving the viewer to experience the café and wonder which overheard conversations are contrived.**
Date/time/location:	**Mon 23 May to Fri 27 May 2:30—3:30pm**
	Four Cousins Grille and Coffee Lounge 10 Market St Arcade Leeds LS1 6DH

Artist(s)/title:	Roland Piché
	The World Trade Center Memorial Competition: A Proposal by Roland Piché
Number/category:	**#30/Festival project**
Description:	**Drawings, maquettes and a film detailing Roland Piché's proposal for a memorial to victims of the 9/11 atrocity. The competition attracted more than five thousand entrants from all over the world, including fifty one from Britain. This exhibition highlights the processes and pitfalls of involvement in such a high-profile event.**
Date/time/location:	**Thurs 12 May to Tues 31 May Mon to Sun 10am—5:30pm Wed 10am—9pm**
	Henry Moore Institute 74 The Headrow Leeds LS1 3AH
	Disabled access available
	0113 246 9469 matthew@henry-moore.ac.uk

Situation Leeds locator map for exhibitions and events.
Plan your route around the festival and use the stickers below to highlight the projects or talks that you want to see. Just peel off a sticker and stick it in the circle shown on each page.
It's an easy way to make sure that you don't miss out on the many enjoyable and interesting experiences at the festival.

Festival locator map

KERR/NOBLE
**Jerwood Furniture
Prize Catalog**

Art Director:
Kerr/Noble
Designer:
Kerr/Noble
Client:
Crafts Council

GOLLINGS
& PIDGEON
**The Plot
Thickens Catalog**

Art Director:
David Pidgeon
Designer:
Marianna Berek-Lewis
Client:
Heide Museum of
Modern Art
Software:
QuarkXPress
Paper/Materials:
Freelife Vellum White,
Encore Super Gloss
Recycled

THE PLOT
THICKENS

NARRATIVES IN
AUSTRALIAN ART

A HEIDE MUSEUM OF MODERN ART
TRAVELLING EXHIBITION

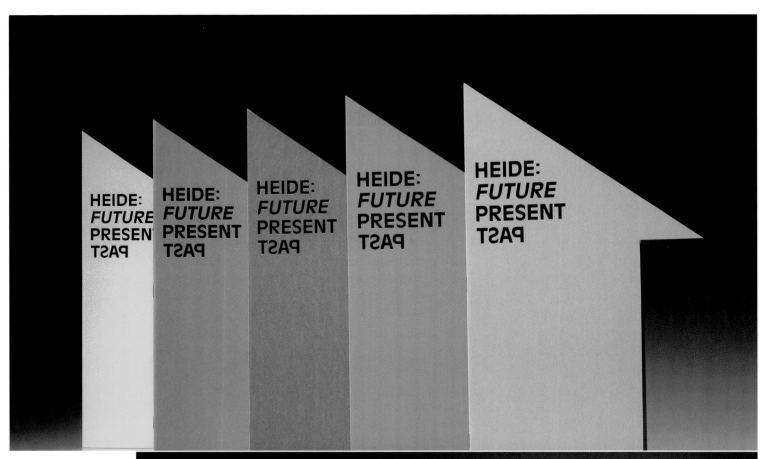

GOLLINGS
& PIDGEON
**Future Present
Past Catalog**

Art Director:
David Pidgeon
Designer:
Tina Chen
Client:
Heide Museum of
Modern Art
Software:
Adobe InDesign
Paper/Materials:
Optix: Inga Turquoise,
Suni Yellow, Janz
Orange, Reva Green,
Raza Red, Monza
Satin Recycled

SAS DESIGN
Awards Catalog

Art Directors:
Christine Fent,
Hanja Hellpap,
Gilmar Wendt
Designers:
Christine Fent,
Hanja Hellpap,
Gilmar Wendt
Client:
STD
Software:
QuarkXPress
Paper/Materials:
Hanno Art Matt

SAS DESIGN
**BT Connected
Worlds Arts
Project Madrid**

Art Director:
Gilmar Wendt
Designer:
Rosanna Vitiello
Client:
BT
Software:
QuarkXPress
Paper/Materials:
Colorplan Plain
Finish Pristine White
(cover), Munken
Print Extra Vol 18
Parilux Gloss (text)

¿Para qué necesitamos el arte en las ciudades? Un recorrido histórico permite decir que las artes, y en general los recursos estéticos, son necesarios no sólo por razones ornamentales sino en otros sentidos más decisivos. Encuentro al menos cuatro fines con los cuales el arte, la literatura y los medios masivos han intervenido e intervienen en espacios urbanos: para fundarlos y refundarlos, para celebrar, para espectacularizar y para nombrar u ocultar su pérdida. Néstor García Canclini

Why do we need art in cities? If we look at history we can see that the arts, and aesthetic resources in general, are necessary not just for ornamental purposes but also for more important reasons. I can identify at least four motivating factors which underlie the continuing intervention of art, literature and the mass media in urban spaces: to create and recreate these spaces, to celebrate them, to make them more spectacular, and to pinpoint or conceal their loss. Néstor García Canclini

PENTAGRAM DESIGN,
SAN FRANCISCO
AIGA Design Legends Gala Program

Art Director:
Kit Hinrichs
Designer:
Jessica Siegel
Client:
AIGA
Software:
Adobe InDesign
Paper/Materials:
Sappi McCoy, Cougar

The Design Legends Gala is a nascent tradition, in only its second year, and already a celebratory occasion for all who respect the importance of the great design legacy. The gala is an opportunity for the community of designers to gather and honor those who have come before and whose creativity, inspiration, innovation and brilliant execution have defined the profession and every young designer's ambitions. This is an event where old friendships are renewed, new friendships are created and everyone is in awe of the sheer talent of the design profession.

ARTS, ENTERTAINMENT, AND EVENT BROCHURES 325

RB-M
**Suky Best/
Artist's Publication**

Designer:
Richard
Bonner-Morgan
Client:
Film & Video Umbrella
Software:
QuarkXPress
Paper/Materials:
Neptune Unique,
Fenner Paper

Ó!
Newsletter for FIT

Art Director:
Einar Gylfason
Designer:
Einar Gylfason
Client:
FIT, Association of
Icelandic Graphic
Designers
Software:
Freehand
Paper/Materials:
California duo 400 gr,
Z-opaque W type R
50 gr

EXPERIMENTAL
JETSET
Time and Again

Art Director:
Experimental Jetset
Designer:
Experimental Jetset
Client:
Stedelijk Museum

LSD
Promotional Pamphlets for an Art Gallery

Art Directors:
Sonia Díaz,
Gabriel Martínez
Designers:
Sonia Díaz,
Gabriel Martínez
Client:
Centroarte
Software:
Adobe Photoshop,
Freehand
Paper/Materials:
Offset on different
papers

¿Cómo puede ocurrir que lo que subyuga nuestra imaginación, disguste a nuestros ojos? DIDEROT

La primera vez que abordé la obra de EB ·ahora hace un año· realicé algunas consideraciones sobre el ascetismo de su mirada, que limitaba los materiales y reducía los elementos puestos en juego en su trabajo pictórico.

Me llamó la atención su texto explicativo "Apuntes sobre pespuntes", en el que mostraba la capacidad de reflexionar sobre su propia obra y en el que aludía a un cierto grado cero barthesiano de su trabajo, como un proceso abierto y en revisión. Frente a la tentación creciente del exceso expresivo y de la acumulación de significados, me llamó poderosamente la atención ese ejercicio de contención que emparenta con la sentencia de Mies van der Rohe "Less is more". Navegar hoy, además, en aguas de la abstracción geométrica en tiempos presididos por otros rumbos neofigurativos o por otros rumbos sin norte alguno, era, tal vez, un síntoma de osadía marinera o un propósito descabellado, que no restaban rigor y misterio a un proceso en formación y a un trabajo enraizado en las experiencias de los Neoplasticistas holandeses y en los Suprematistas soviéticos de la segunda década del siglo.

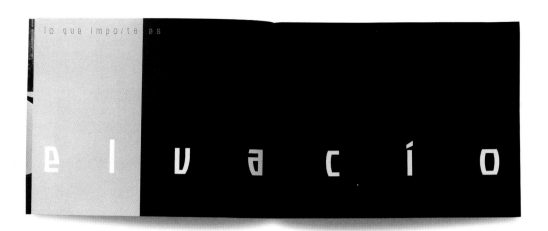

lo que importa es

el vacío

LSD
**Artist's
Promotional
Brochure**

Art Directors:
Sonia Díaz,
Gabriel Martínez
Designers:
Sonia Díaz,
Gabriel Martínez
Client:
Eduardo Barco
Software:
Adobe Photoshop,
Freehand
Paper/Materials:
Offset

what is important is

emptiness

LSD
**Brochure for a
Country Hotel**

Art Director:
Gabriel Martínez
Designer:
Gabriel Martínez
Client:
El Milano Real
Software:
Freehand
Paper/Materials:
Offset

Anchor Graphics

Anchor Graphics works in the areas of visual arts and arts education for youth, adult, and professional artists. We are a community-based nonprofit printshop and gallery that brings together, under professional guidance, a diverse community of youth, emerging and established artists, and the public to advance the fine art of printmaking by integrating education with the creation of prints. For over fourteen years, Anchor Graphics has offered educational programs, exhibitions, and artist services revolving around the history and practice of printmaking. Anchor Graphics is a printshop, which functions as both a classroom and an atelier, fulfilling the need for affordable access to a properly equipped shop, while maintaining a focus on education within a professional artistic environment. As a non-profit organization, our ethos is three-fold. First, Anchor Graphics maintains an environment in which artists of all experience and age levels are welcome, encouraged to explore and be innovative with the printmaking medium, and supported in realizing their own creative visions. We offer open studio time that allows artists of various skill levels to work under the guidance of master printers, and an Artist-in-Residency program that brings experienced artist/printmakers from across the country to Chicago to share

their knowledge and work. Second, Anchor Graphics mentors Chicagoland area youth. By introducing them to printmaking and educating them in the discipline through Press-On-Wheels workshops and high school classes, we are equipping them with fundamental life tools. Through the creation of original images and the running of professional hand presses we are teaching young people the value of cooperation and sequential planning. All of our high school classes and workshops are free to the students. We also hire interns from various colleges every year and train them in all aspects of running a nonprofit printshop and gallery. Finally, we are committed to educating the community at large about printmaking. Through exhibitions, lectures, demonstrations, and adult classes we are making this art form accessible to anyone who wishes to learn about printmaking's process and history.

FIREBELLY DESIGN
Artist/Nonprofit Brochure

Art Director:
Dawn Hancock
Designers:
Dawn Hancock,
Brent Maynard
Client:
Anchor Graphics/JET
Software:
Adobe Photoshop,
Adobe Illustrator,
Adobe InDesign
Paper/Materials:
Sappi McCoy Velvet

RUSSELL
WARREN-FISHER
21 Years of
Complicite

Designer:
Russell Warren-Fisher
Client:
Complicite
Software:
QuarkXPress,
Adobe Photoshop

NB:STUDIO
What Is Craft?

Art Directors:
Nick Finney, Ben Stott,
Alan Dye
Designer:
Jodie Whiteman
Client:
The Hub

NB:STUDIO
Schweppes
Photographic
Portrait Prize

Art Directors:
Nick Finney, Ben Stott,
Alan Dye
Designer:
Ian Pierce
Client:
National Portrait
Gallery

Schweppes
Photographic
Portrait
Prize 2003

"Architecture need do nothing more than assist man's homecoming."

「建築所要做的事，無非就是讓居住者多一份回家的溫暖感覺。」

STUDIO
MYERSCOUGH
Hometime

Art Director:
Morag Myerscough
Designer:
Morag Myerscough
Photographer:
Richard Learoyd
Client:
British Council

新居家时代
英国当代居家设计展

WHY NOT
ASSOCIATES
Nike City Knife

Client:
Nike UK
Software:
Freehand MX

PENTAGRAM
DESIGN, BERLIN
**Mozarthaus Vienna
Program**

Art Director:
Justus Oehler
Designers:
Justus Oehler,
Josephine Rank
Client:
Mozarthaus Vienna
Software:
QuarkXPress
Paper/Materials:
Munken Lynx

Raquel Ormella

Shaun Gladwell

BOCCALATTE
C Town Bling Catalog

Art Director:
Suzanne Boccalatte
Client:
Campbelltown Arts Centre
Software:
Adobe Creative Suite
Paper/Materials:
Monza Foil Stamp

mattress is a threshold to sleep upon /
a strange quilted force / of softening
matters / and everlasting springs /
a cushion for the body's travels through
the times of night / at whichever
hour / off the ground / off the floor /
a place for yonder life / an island
for refuge and panic and trauma and
fatigue / a site of unimagined grief and
imagined love / a thing / an artful
object for flesh and blood and thought
to spread like animals / adrift / falling
from nowhere in divine-particular /
just here / this moment / falling into
rage or calm / eyes closed and seeing /
infinite operas / wondrous vistas /
delicate gifts subtle dangers embracing
voids / dying for hours / or maybe not /
instead / wide-awake / nerve ends
razor-sharp / feverish / the ill or joyful
creature gushes leaks seeps moults
rubs squeezes / leaving itself like a
ghost on the surface and more ghostly
still below the surface / on the mythical
heart of the thing's patience / its exact
presence / weight depth length width /
the body descends willingly / becomes
threshold too / abandoning its own
heart-dream / each laboured mattress
made of earth substances pulled to
light / for unprecedented passioned and
dispassioned touches / the mattress-
cosmos awaits something-to-come / and
it does / birth / death / and every minute
betwixt state / even now at this late
hour / an image of it / refuge as refuse /
excessive in its worn broken luxuriance /
a desert / deserted / recorded /
presented / simply saying 'I am'

VOICE
**Photographic
Exhibition Catalog**

Art Director:
Scott Carslake
Designer:
Scott Carslake
Client:
Toby Richardson
Software:
Adobe InDesign,
Photoshop
Paper/Materials:
Paper by Daltons,
Process Color, Saddle
Stitch

Teresa's story
'We miss our mother'
**Nkwazi compound
Ndola, Zambia**

Teresa died on 6 May 2001, just three months after this photograph was taken for Cold Heaven. Her two children, Aaron and Mavis, were ten and eight years old. They still cry at night.

'We miss our mother,' Aaron says quietly. 'She looked after us and brought us food and clothes. When she was ill, we swept the house, washed the clothes and fetched water. We liked looking after her because she was our mother.'

When Don McCullin gave Aaron this photograph, he turned away, overcome, his face in his hands. Aaron had never seen a photograph of his mother. Today it stands framed, in pride of place, on the dresser.

'I am sure Aaron has had dreams of his mother,' said McCullin. 'He must have thought for a second that he had been living a nightmare for the past three years and that she was actually there which he saw that photo.'

The children are lucky to have found a loving and secure home with their paternal grandparents, Margaret, 62, and Oteshi, 66. The children's father, their only son, died of an HIV-related disease in 2001.

On the day McCullin arrived, they were eating leftover grains of dried maize for breakfast. Oteshi earns 40 pence/60 cents a day as a cobbler. The family cannot afford the Zambian staple of maize porridge. Although a community organisation pays for the children's schooling, the family has to pay for the water the children collect from a standpipe each day; water services are privatised in Zambia. Often they go to bed hungry.

'But we are happy, praise the Lord,' says Margaret. 'We have lost our only son and now we have the grandchildren to replace him.'

'When I look at Teresa's picture she comes across as strangely beautiful and quietly courageous – a woman who could barely move and yet was bringing up two children.'

Don McCullin

die of HIV

ans

people

cent of people p get it

ments 6 billion

Life Interrupted
Don McCullin
HIV/AIDS in Africa

Foreword by Joan Bakewell

Christian Aid

LIPPA PEARCE
"Life Interrupted" Catalog for Don McCulin Exhibition

Art Director:
Harry Pearce
Designer:
Harry Pearce
Client:
Christian Aid

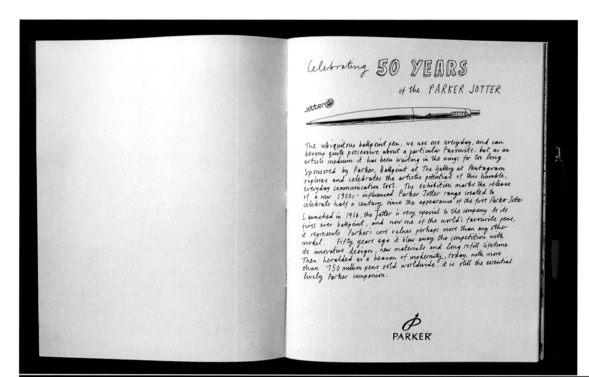

PENTAGRAM
DESIGN, LONDON
Ballpoint

Art Director:
Angus Hyland
Client:
Parker Pens

ATELIER WORKS
RSA House Guide

Art Director:
Ian Chilvers
Designer:
Ian Chilvers
Client:
Royal Society of Arts
Software:
QuarkXPress

directory of contributors

2D3D
Mauritskade 1
Den Haag 2514 HC, The Netherlands

300 Million
1 Rosoman Place
London EC1R OJY, UK

After Hours Creative
5444 E. Washington, Suite 3
Phoenix, AZ 85034

Ajans Ultra
Aslan Yatagis.Feza ap.33/1/12, 80060 Cihangir
Istanbul 80060, Turkey

Allegro 168
150 Cathcart Street
Ottawa, Ontario K1N 5B8, Canada

Allemann Almquist & Jones
301 Cherry Street, 3rd floor
Philadelphia, PA 19106

Aloof Design
5 Fisher Street
Lewes, East Sussex, BN7 2DG, UK

Alterpop
1001 Mariposa Street #204
San Francisco, CA 94107

And Partners
158 West 27th Street Floor 7
New York, NY 10001

Antfarm Inc.

Arias Associates
502 Waverley Street
Palo Alto, CA 94301

Aspen Interactive
7036 Park Drive
New Port Richey, FL 34652

Atelier Works
The Old Piano Factory, 5 Charlton Kings Road
London NW5 2SB, UK

Bakken Creative Co.
801 Clay Street
Oakland, CA 94607

Bandujo Donker & Brothers
22 West 19th Street, 9th floor
New York, NY 10011

BBK Studio
648 Monroe NW, Suite 212
Grand Rapids, MI 49503

BC, MH James Lambert
32 Sunbury Workshops, Swanfield St
London E2 7LF, UK

Billy Blue Creative, Precinct
PO Box 728 North Sydney
NSW 2059, Australia

Bisqit Design
5 Theobalds Road
London WC1X 8SH, UK

Blackletter Design Inc.
Wigan Road, Ashton-in-Marketfield
Wigan, WN4 9SU Manchester, UK

Bloch + Coulter Design Group
2440 S. Sedelveda Blvd. #152
Los Angeles, CA 90064

Blok Design
822 Richmond Street West, Suite 301
Toronto, ON M6J 1C9, Canada

Boccalatte
Studio 43.61 Marlborough Street
Surrey Hills, Sydney, NSW 2010, Australia

Bolt
1415 South Church Street
Charlotte, NC 28227

Brunazzi & Associati
22 Via Andorno
Torino, 10153 Italy

Buro 7
Humboldstrasse 64
Bremen 28203, Germany

Cacao Design

Cahan & Associates
171 Second Street, 5th floor
San Francisco, CA 94105

Cartlidge Levene
238 St Johns Street
EC1V 4PH London, UK

Cem Erutku Tasarim Studyosu
Tarilk Zafer Tunayasok
3/6 Gunussuyu, Istanbol, Turkey

CF Napa

Cheng Design
University of Washington, box 353440, art
    building room 102
Seattle, WA 98195

Clarity Coverdale Fury
120 South 6th Street, Suite 1300
Minneapolis, MN 55402

Clark Creative Group
251 Rhode Island Street #204
San Francisco, CA 94103

Country Companies Design Services
1711 GE Road
Blooming, IL 61701

Cox Design
5196 Hummingbird Road
Pleasanton, CA 94566

Creative Conspiracy, Inc.
862 Main Avenue, Suite 850
Durango, CO 81301

Cross Colours Ink
8 Eastwood Road
Dunkeld West 2196 Johannesburg,
    South Africa

CSAA Creative Services
100 Van Ness Avenue
San Francisco, CA 94102

Design Asylum PTE LTD
46B Club Street
Singapore 069423

Design Project
Round Foundry Media Centre, Unit G15,
    Foundry St
Leeds LS11 5QP, UK

Dinnick & Howells
2943 Markham Street
Toronto, Ontario M6J 296, Canada

Doppio Design
25 Rosemary Avenue, Oranjezicht
Cape Town 8001 South Africa

Dowling Design & Art Direction
Navigation House, 48 Millgate
Newark, NG24 4TS, UK

Edelman Public Relations Worldwide
636 Broadway Suite 707
New York, NY 10012

Elfen
Ty Meandros, 54A Bute Street
Cardiff Bay CF10 5A5, UK

Emerson, Wajdowicz Studios
1123 Broadway, Suite 1106
New York, NY 10010

Emery Vincent Design
15 Foster Street, level 1, Surrey Hills
Sydney NSW 2010, Australia

Erbe Design
1500 Oxley Street
South Pacadena, CA 91030

Experimental JetSet
Jan Hanzenstraat 37, 1st floor
1053 SK Amsterdam, The Netherlands

Fabio Ongarato Design
569 Church Street
Richmond, Victoria 3121, Australia

Fauxpas
Hardturmstrasse.261
Zurich CH 8005, Switzerland

Firebelly Design
2701 W Thomas, 2nd floor
Chicago, IL 60622

Fitch
10350 Olentangy River Road
Worthington, OH 43085

Flight Creative
117.5 S. Union Street
Traverse City, MI 49684

Flore Van Ryn
7 Rue de la Seconde Reine
1180 Bruxelles, Belgium

Foco Media gmbh & cte
Spitzwegstr 6
Munich 81373 Germany

Fork Unstable Media GMBH
Juliusstrasse 25
Hamburg 22769, Germany

Form
47 Tabernacle Street
London EC2A 4AA, UK

Fossil
2280 N. Greenville Avenue
Richardson, TX 750082

Frost Design
The Gymnasium, Kings Way Place
Sans Walk, London EC1R 0LU, UK

Fuszion Collaborative
901 Prince Street
Alexandria, VA 22314

Gee + Chung Design
38 Bryant Street, Suite 100
San Francisco, CA 94105

Giorgio Rocco Communications
Via Domenichino 27
Milano 20149 Italy

Gollings & Pidgeon
147 Chapel Street
St. Kilda, Victoria, Australia

Graif Design
165 E. Highway CC
Nixa, MO 65714

Graphiculture
322 1st Avenue North, Suite 500
Minneapolis, MN 55401

Greenzweig Design
600 First Avenue, Suite 330
Seattle, WA 98104

Greteman Group
142 North Mosley
Wichita, KS 67202

Hallmark Loyalty
2501 Mcgee Street, Drop 19
Kansas City, MO 64108

Hand Made Group
Sartori, 16
52017 Stia, Italy

Hangar 18 Creative Group
220-137 West 3rd Avenue
Vancouver, BC, V6J 1K7, Canada

Hartford Design, Inc
954 W. Washington, 4th floor
Chicago, IL 60607

Hatch Creative
Suite 1, 147 Chapel Street, St Kilda
Melbourne, Victoria 3182, Australia

Hat-Trick Design
Studio 11, Clink Street Studios
1 Clink Street, London SE1, UK

Hebe.Werbung & Design
Magstadterstrasse 12
Leonberg 71229, Germany

HGV
2-6 Northburgh Street
London EC1V 0AY, UK

Hippo Studio
58 Queen's Road East
Wanchai, Hong Kong

Hornall Anderson Design Works, Inc.
1008 Western Avenue, Suite 600
Seattle, WA 98104

Howry Design Associates
354 Pine Street, #600
San Francisco, CA 94104

Huddleston Malone Design
56 Exchange Place
Salt Lake City, UT 84111

IAAH
727 Duffosat Street
New Orleans, LA 70115

ICO Design Consultancy
75-77 Great Portland Street
London W1W 7CR, UK

IE Design
1600 Rosecrans Avenue, Building 6B
Manhatten Beach, CA 90266

Imelda Agency
Poljanska cesta 25
SI-1000 Ljubljana, Slovenija

Inaria
270 Lafayette Street, Suite 906
New York, NY 10012

INOX Design
Via Terraggio II
Milan, Italy

Iridium
43 Eccles Street, 2nd floor
Ottawa, ON K1R 653, Canada

Kamper Brands
510 Washington Avenue, South
Minneapolis, MN 55415

Kan & Lau Design Consultants
28/F Great Smart Tower,
230 Wanchai Road, Hong Kong

Kerr/Noble
Studio 53, Pennybank Chambers
33-35 St. John's Square, London EC1M 4DS

Kesselskramer
Lauriegracht 39
Amsterdam 1016 RG, The Netherlands

Kinetic Singapore
2 Leng Kee Road Thye, Hong Centre
#04-03A Singapore 159086, Singapore

KO Creation
6300 Park Avenue, Suite 420
Montreal, QC H2V 2H8,Canada

Kolegram
37 St. Joseph Boulevard
Gatineau Quebec J8Y 3V8, Canada

LA Weekly
6715 Sunset Boulevard
Los Angeles, CA 90028

Lava Graphic Designers
Van Diemenstraat 366
1013CR Amsterdam, The Netherlands

Lead Dog Digital
245 E 25th Street 3J
New York, NY 10012

Lee Reedy Creative
1542 Williams Street
Denver, CO 80218

Lippa Pearce
358A Richmond Road
Twickenham TW1 2DU, UK

Liska & Associates, Inc
515 North State Street, 23rd floor
Chicago, IL 60610

Lloyds Graphic Design LTD
17 West 107th Street, apt 5W
New York, NY 10025

Lorenz Advertising
9320 Chesapeake Drive, #214
San Diego, CA 92123

Louey/Rubino Design Group Inc.
2525 Main Street, Suite 204
Santa Monica, CA 90405

Lowercase, Inc.
213 W. Institute Place, Suite 311
Chicago, IL 60610

LSD
San Andres, 36 2o P6
Madrid 28004, Spain

Made Thought
181 Cannon St Rd, 2nd floor
London E1 2LX, UK

Marius Fahrner Design
Suttnerstrasse 8
Hamburg 22767, Germany

Melissa Passehl Design
1275 Lincoln Avenue, Suite 7
San Jose, CA 95125

Metal
1210 West Clay Suite 17
Houston, TX 77019

Michael Courtney Design
121 East Boston
Seattle, WA 98102

Michael Patrick Partners
532 Emerson Street
Palo Alto, CA 94301

Michal Granit Design Studio
P.O. Box 303
Sdeh Varburg, 44935, Israel

Mike Lackersteen Design
35 Rochester Square
London NW1 9RZ, UK

Miriello Grafico Inc.
419 West 6 Street
San Diego, CA 92101, UK

Mirko Ilic Corp.
207 East 32nd Street
New York, NY 10016

Monster Design
3022 Commerce Street
Dallas, TX 75226

Musuem of Fine Arts, Boston
465 Huntington Avenue
Boston, MA 02215

Mutabor Design
Barnerstrasse 63/HOF
Hamburg 22765, Germany

Mytton Williams
15 St. James's Parade
Bath BA1 1UL, UK

NB: Studio
24 Store Street
London WC1E 7BA, UK

Nesnadny & Schwartz
10803 Magnolia Drive
Cleveland, OH 44106

Net Integrators - Net Design
Post Box 59016
Amsterdam 1040 KA, The Netherlands

Nina David KommunikationsDesign
Nierderkassler Kirchweg 56
Duesseldorf 40547, Germany

No.Parking

O!
Armuli 11
Reykjavik 108, Iceland

Oden Marketing and Design
22 N. Street, Suite 300
Memphis, TN 38103

Oh Boy, A Design Company
49 Geary Street, Suite 530
San Francisco, CA 94108

Palmquist Creative
P.O. Box 325
Bozeman, MT 59771

Paula Kelly Design
164 Fifth Avenue
New York, NY 10010

Pentagram Design/ Berlin
Leibnizstrasse 60
Berlin 10629, Germany

Pentagram Design/ London
11 Needham Road
London W11 2RP, UK

Pentagram Design/SF
387 Tehama Street
San Francisco, CA 94103

Pepe Gimeno- Proyecto Grafico
C/Cadiers, s.n. Pol. D'Oradors
Godella, Valencia E-46110, Spain

Perks Design Partners

Ping-Pong Design
Rochussenstraat 400
3015 ZC Rotterdam, The Netherlands

Popcorn Initiative
1602 Robin Road
Orlando, FL 32803

Poulin + Morris
286 Springs Street, 6th floor
New York, NY 10013

Q
Sonnenbergerstrasse 16
Wiesbaden 65193, Germany

Radley Yeldar
326 City Road
London ECN 2SP, UK

RB-M
100 De Beauvoir Road
London N1 4EN, UK

Rose Design Associates
30 Great Guildford Street
London SE1 0HS, UK

Russell Warren-Fisher
Beech House, Bradford Road
Hawthorn, Wiltshire, UK

Ruth Huimerind

Sagenvier Design Kommunikation
Sagerstrasse 4
6850 Dornbirn, Vorarlberg, Austria

Sagmeister Inc.
222 West 14 Street
New York, NY 10011

Salterbaxter
8 Teleford Road
London W10 5SH , UK

SamataMason, Inc.
101 South First Street
Des Plaines, IL 60016

SAS Design
6 Salem Road
London W2 4BU, UK

Sayles Graphic Design
3701 Beaver Avenue
Des Moines, IA 50310

SEA
70 St John Street
London EC1M 4DT, UK

Segura Inc.
1110 North Milwaukee Avenue
Chicago, IL 60622

Shamlian Advertising
10 E. Sprout Road
Springfield, PA 19064

Sibley Peteet Design
1409 South Lemar, Suite 234
Dallas, TX 75215

Squires & Company
2913 Canton Street
Dallas, TX 75226

Stilradar
Schwabstr. 10a
70197 Stuttgart, Germany

Stoltze Design
15 Channel Center Street #603
Boston, MA 02210

Studio Myerscough
26 Drysdale Street
London N1 6LS, UK

Subplot Design Inc.
301-308 Homer Street
Vancouver, BC V6B 2V2, Canada

Taxi Studio LTD
93 Princess Victoria Street
Clifton, Bristol BS8 4DD, UK

The Bonsey Design Partnership
179 River Valley Road
Singapore 179033

The Chase
1 North Parade, Parsonage Gardens
Manchester M3 2NH, UK

The Kitchen
52-53 Margaret Street
London W1W 8SQ, UK

The Point Group

Together Design
106 Cleveland Street
London W1T 6NX, UK

Tracy Design Communications, Inc.
118 S.W. Boulevard
Kansas City, MO 64108

Trickett & Webb Ltd.
The Factory, 84 Marchmont Street
London, WCIN IAG England, UK

Tycoon Graphics
402 Villa Gloria 2-13-7 Jingumae, Shibuya-ku
Tokyo 150-0001 Japan

University of Iowa Foundation
One West Park Road
Iowa City, IA 52244-4550

Usine De Boutons
Via Guido Franco 99/B Cadoneghe
Padova 35010, Italy

Vine360
50 N 4th Ave #18B
Minneapolis, MN 55401

Vinje Design Inc
1043 Contra Costa Drive
El Cerrito, CA 94530

Viva Dolan Communications and Design
99 Crown's Lane, Suite 500
Toronto, Ontario M5R 3P4, Canada

Voice
217 Gilbert Street
Adelaide, South Australia, 5000 Australia

Weymouth Design
332 Congress St
Boston, MA 02210

Why Not Associates
22c Sheoherdess Walk
London N1 7LB, UK

Willboughby Design Group
602 Westport Road
Kansas City, MO 64111

William Homan Design
1316 West 73rd Street
Minneapolis, MN 55423

Zappata Disenadores S.C.
Lafayete 143 Apzunes 11590
Mexico City, Mexico

Zucchini Design PTE LTD
28A Mosque St
Singapore 059506

index